THE ISLE OF MAN

No holiday island is more popular than the Isle of Man. Since watering places began to be frequented some two hundred years ago, millions of visitors from the mainland and Ireland have found it a welcome escape from everyday life. It is beautiful and offers virtually every facility for leisure activity.

This guide describes the resort in a way that will enhance the pleasure of a visit before and after the occasion. It covers all aspects of the island—its fascinating history, scenery and topography and the many activities that can be enjoyed in this semi-independent 'country' which has moved with the times but has managed to retain its old charm for immigrant resident and tourist alike.

THE ISLANDS SERIES

*Published in the United States by Stackpole
Other titles published in the United States by David & Charles Inc
The series is distributed in Australia by Wren Publishing Pty Ltd, Melbourne

THE ISLE OF MAN

by H. S. CORRAN

DAVID & CHARLES

NEWTON ABBOT   LONDON   NORTH POMFRET (VT)   VANCOUVER

ISBN 0 7153 7417 6

Set in 11 on 13pt Monotype Baskerville
and printed in Great Britain
by Latimer Trend & Company Ltd Plymouth
for David & Charles (Publishers) Limited
Brunel House Newton Abbot Devon

Published in the United States of America
by David & Charles Inc
North Pomfret Vermont 05053 USA

Published in Canada
by Douglas David & Charles Limited
1875 Welch Street North Vancouver BC

CONTENTS

Topographical

INTRODUCTION

THE eminent geographer Mackinder likened the Irish Sea to 'a British Mediterranean—a land-girt quadrilateral whose four sides are England, Scotland, Ireland and Wales. The mountains of all four are visible from Snaefell—the peak which rises from the midst of the Irish Sea to a height of 2,000ft, forming the summit of the Isle of Man, a fifth part of the British Isles, neither English, Scottish, Irish, nor Welsh, but Manx.'

The Isle of Man is indeed the nearest community to the mean centre of the British Isles. The northern tip of the island is just under 20 miles from Burrow Head in Wigtownshire, Scotland; about 32 miles from St Bees Head, in Cumbria, England; Peel, on the west coast is about 32 miles from the Irish coast of County Down, and the Calf of Man in the south is about 45 miles from the coast of Anglesey in North Wales.

In the two centuries since watering places began to be frequented millions of visitors, almost entirely from the four surrounding countries, have landed in the Isle of Man and found it in so many ways a welcome escape from their everyday life. For over a century, the tourist industry has been the main economic activity of the island. The chief mode of transport has naturally been by sea, and even today air travel accounts for only a third of total arrivals. A regular ferry service has been in existence between Liverpool and Douglas, the island's largest town, since 1830 and this is still the way the majority of visitors come. The journey down the Mersey Channel to the Bar light vessel takes about an hour, and the ship then turns north-west towards the island:

7

How gaily and quickly the time passes. Groups of twos and threes saunter leisurely up and down the deck, or lean lazily on the sides of the vessel, gazing at the shining water and the far-off ships . . . What is that, like a summer cloud, rising out of the sea? It is the first glimpse of our destination, the Isle of Man; and quickly the summer cloud resolves itself into something more substantial than vapour as the hills and general outline of the Manx coast become more distinct.

Soon the bay of Douglas opens out before you, a beautiful picture framed in by hills and headlands, standing out in purple shadows against the summer sky. The mountains stretch in a continuous chain along the horizon and their sunlit slopes are diversified by the shadowy valleys which intersect them. On the left hand, Douglas Head rises steeply, 300ft high . . . on the right, in the distance, Banks' Howe stretches far into the sea, a bold high promontory, along which, in winter, the waves break in never ceasing fury. Between these encircling arms lies the beautiful crescent-shaped bay of Douglas. Fine promenades fringe the shoreline, along which we see people and carriages moving. Behind these rise the spires and roofs of the town, mounting to the top of the low hills on which Douglas is built . . . in the foreground, standing a little distance from the mainland, is an islet with its miniature Tower of Refuge.

This description, from the Isle of Man Steam Packet Company's *Guide Book*, which appeared regularly during the present century until 1939, sums up the visitor's first view of the island. Today the picture has changed little. Douglas Head, beside the castellated hotel which has stood for a century, now boasts a radio station and on Banks' Howe the creeping tide of suburban housing is steadily encroaching on the once unsullied green slopes.

After sailing into it for a lifetime, Douglas Bay continues to be an exciting prospect from the sea—none the less so on those occasions when the weather is not so beneficent and heavy seas hurl themselves across it from the south-west. The promenade has been developed and is well cared for; the boarding houses and hotels which lie along its length are brightly painted, while the style of architecture, unremarkable half a century ago, is becoming more attractive with age.

The 30 per cent of visitors who arrive by air land at Ronaldsway, near Castletown, about 8 miles south of Douglas. For obvious reasons the airport is situated on the low-lying coastal platform which occupies this corner of the island; a bus whisks the new arrival along a fast road into Douglas in twenty minutes.

For the visitor from Britain there is no immediate impression of being in a strange land. A distinctive local accent exists but is less in evidence in modern times for various reasons; much less is there a live native language, as in Wales, though efforts are being made to introduce Manx street names. The island has its own coinage, but British coins and notes are universally accepted, as indeed are those from the Republic of Ireland. Branches of UK chain stores and banks are found in the main streets; the Isle of Man's own bank is now part of one of the British banking groups. The local radio station, Radio Manx, is in its own way a pioneer. Television is available by a relay system —the BBC mast being on Douglas Head, the ITV at Richmond Hill, south of Douglas—but many people receive their programmes direct from transmissions in the north of England or Northern Ireland.

Although the Isle of Man has been associated with the survival of such archaic forms of transport as the mountain railway or the horse tram, the paramount form of communication is now by road. Four car-ferry vessels busily transport private cars and small vans from Liverpool, winter and summer, and from other ports such as Ardrossan, Belfast and Dublin during the summer months. The island has for nearly seventy years been a magnet for motor cyclists because of its association with the famous Manx Tourist Trophy Races, which have continued without a break, apart from wartime, since 1907.

The high density of motor car ownership soon becomes obvious. Even in the depths of winter Douglas has a parking problem. If Douglas is the first glimpse of the Isle of Man for most arrivals, it is by no means the whole. The island is 30 miles long from south-west to north-east and 10 miles wide on average. With good roads available, the visitor can drive round the perimeter in half a day. This tour would reveal that the main towns and villages are dotted round the edge of a central upland massif. Peel and Port Erin lie on the west coast, and Douglas, Ramsey, Laxey, Castletown and Port St Mary on the east. North of Ramsey, the most northerly town of any size, the countryside changes dramatically, rock and mountain giving way to flat plain and sand dunes, more reminiscent of Norfolk.

On a reasonably clear day, the Cumberland coast may be seen from almost any point between Douglas and Ramsey; from the northernmost point—the Point of Ayre—Wigtownshire is visible on all but the haziest days, and from Peel it is possible to see County Down, in Northern Ireland. In good visibility North Wales may be discerned even from Douglas, though this is not so common.

In recent years, the island has become a desirable place of residence and a tax haven. After a long period of decline, the population has started to increase—not because of the fertility of the inhabitants, but as a result of the immigration of thousands of newcomers. This has led to a shortage of houses, and many old cottages, once almost derelict, have been converted into modern dwellings. The island has a well-cared-for look. It has nevertheless retained its old charm, with a great variety of scenery, the ever-recurring motif of sea and sky, the dark glens with bubbling streams, the open moorlands on the mountainsides, and the quaint old twisted streets of Peel and Castletown.

1   NATURAL FEATURES

THE Isle of man lies roughly NNE/SSW along its major axis, with a diagonal range of mountains running north-east to south-west. This divides the island into two regions, one with a south-easterly aspect towards England and Wales, and the other facing north-west to Scotland and Ireland. The eastern slopes tend to be more gentle than those on the western side. In the south-east the slopes merge into descending levels on a bed of limestone; in the north there is a very steep descent on to a wide alluvial plain. This lends some variety to the scenery, though inevitably the scarcity of trees leads to a general appearance of bare hills and fenced fields. The island covers an area of about 227sq miles, or 145,000 acres.

There are three smaller off-shore islands. The largest is the Calf of Man, off the southern tip, between Port Erin and Port St Mary. St Patrick's Isle at Peel, on which the castle and cathedral stand, and St Michael's Isle, at the northern end of the Langness Peninsula flanking Derbyhaven, are now connected by causeway to the main island.

MOUNTAINS AND RIVERS

The mountain range terminates in the north with North Barrule, 1,854ft ('Barrule' is derived from 'Wardfell', the Hill of Watch and Ward—in former times a constant vigil was kept here for possible invasion by sea) and in the south with South Barrule, 1,586ft, and Cronk-ny-Irree-Laa, 1,433ft. The main northern peaks are Snaefell, 2,036ft; Beinn-y-Phott, 1,790ft; Garraghan, 1,640ft; Colden, 1,599ft, and Slieau Freoaghane, 1,601ft; there are numerous others of 1,000–1,500ft. The northern group covers twice as much area as the southern.

The upland massif naturally gives rise to a great number of streams, and on average there is a river entering the sea every 3 miles round the 70-mile coastline. Mostly these flow directly from the central watershed on a straight and often steep course to the sea, but the largest—the Sulby—has a course of 10 miles; after flowing north from the slopes of Snaefell, it turns sharply east to enter the sea at Ramsey. Douglas stands at the confluence of the rivers Dhoo and Glass—the latter, with its major tributary, the Baldwin, covers 8 miles on its way to the coast. The Neb, at the mouth of which Peel lies, also follows a winding course of 8 miles to the western coast. In the south, the most important rivers are the Silverburn, which emerges at Castletown, and Santon Burn.

The mountains of the Isle of Man are, as the result of glacial action, round and relatively smooth, with a basic rock formation of slate. Compared with the uplands of North Wales and the Lake District, there is less exposure of rock and crag; heather covers many of the slopes. The northern upland group falls into two sections, separated by the great glen of the Sulby river: in the eastern group are Snaefell, Beinn-y-Phott and North Barrule; in the western, Slieau Dhoo, Slieau Freoaghane and Sartfell. The range extends southwards by Colden, Slieau Ree and Greeba; the latter slopes steeply down to the central rift valley of the island, which contains the east–west road from Douglas to Peel. This valley splits the upland massif; its southern section stretches from Slieau Whallian, on the south side of the midland valley at St Johns, to South Barrule and Cronk-ny-Irree-Laa. All these southern peaks are in the south-western sector of the island.

The foot of Greeba marks the highest point in the central valley and it is from here that the Dhoo flows east to Douglas,

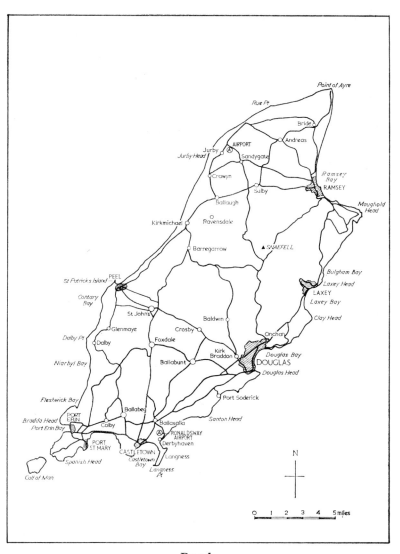

Roads

and a tributary of the Neb eastwards to Peel. The central valley is important to the island's communications, even though the railway no longer runs through it.

The gentle slope of the uplands towards the south-east forms the coastal plateau of the parishes of Arbory, Malew, Castletown, Santon, Braddan and Onchan. On the north side, the fall is much more abrupt and between Ramsey and Kirkmichael the foothills very rapidly give way to the northern plain, comprising the parishes of Kirk Bride, Kirk Andreas, Jurby, Ballaugh, with part of Kirkmichael and Lezayre. The plain extends over 25,000 acres or about one-sixth of the island. It is roughly triangular with the Point of Ayre as its apex, Ramsey at one corner of the base and Orrisdale Head— between Kirkmichael and Ballaugh—at the other.

The larger rivers all rise near the ridge of the upland chain, usually in cols or hollows between mountains: the Glass between Garraghan and Colden, and the Baldwin, a major tributary of the Glass, at the foot of Beinn-y-Phott on the lower slopes of Snaefell; a branch of the Sulby river starts close by but flows north. In the south, the Silverburn rises between Cronk-ny-Irree-Laa and South Barrule, flowing south; while the Glen Rushen river begins a short distance away but flows north and west. The mountain slopes are criss-crossed by smaller or larger tributaries of the main rivers, mostly falling steeply to join the parent stream.

The Sulby has branches which rise west of Snaefell on the northern slopes of Beinn-y-Phott, with major tributaries from Druidale and Glen Crommag which are almost as long as the main branches. Numerous smaller streams join the river along the course of Sulby Glen, two with notable waterfalls. Near the end of its easterly journey to the sea at Ramsey, the Sulby is joined by the Glen Auldyn river. The mouth of the Sulby was formerly a delta with two estuaries, encompassing a delta islet.

Waterfalls are common in Manx glens; the finer ones tend to be on the western side: the Rhenass falls in Glen Helen and the

Glen Meay falls in the Glen Rushen river, though the Dhoon falls, north of Laxey, are also notable.

The northern plain is drained by the Killane and by the Lhen trench, a relatively long—5–6 mile—waterway, reminiscent of the dykes of East Anglia, which has the appearance of being, at least partly, an artefact.

During recorded history, the island's lakes—natural and artificial—have changed considerably. Formerly there were a number of shallow loughs and meres north of Ballaugh; these have now been more or less drained and the area is known as the Curraghs. There was also a chain of narrow loughs along the central rift valley, extending both ways from Greeba. At Ramsey, when the northern mouth of the Sulby was dammed and the land reclaimed, a park lake marked the location. At Injebreck, at the head of the West Baldwin valley and at the source of the river Glass, a reservoir was created which is now one of the beauty spots of the Isle of Man.

ROCKS

The central upland mass of the island may be regarded as an outcropping of the rocks of the English Lake District. These very old slaty rocks, which cover nearly three-quarters of the area, are from primary strata, probably of the Ordovician system. Formed from beds of sediment in seas of the very remote past, they were subsequently raised, hardened and shaped in many ways. The rocks, folded and crushed during the period when the Caledonian mountains were being formed, consist of clay schists, often blue, grey or red; harder gritty rocks, inter stratified with the others, and flaggy greywackes. These rocks outcrop on the higher slopes of the island and their structure may be seen along the east coast, from Langness to Maughold Head. The schists lie at various angles—at Spanish Head in the south, for instance, they are nearly horizontal.

Underneath the primary rocks lies the primeval granite,

outcrops of which occur at Dhoon and Foxdale in particular, and also at Oatlands, south of Douglas. In other places the rock mass was penetrated by veins of molten material, forming dykes where mineralisation occurred. Along the strike of the schists from south-west to north-east are veins of quartz; blocks of this stone were found in early burial cairns.

As well as the movements of upheaval, there has been considerable intense lateral pressure in the rocks. This has given rise, in particular, to the Chasms, near Spanish Head, formed by a lateral movement, not yet finished, whereby blocks of the strata have been pushed on a sloping underbed. The Chasms are vertical clefts between rock masses detaching themselves from the hill. The Sugar Loaf is an isolated and detached example of one of these masses.

The Manx slate beds are about 2,000ft thick and with a notable absence of fossils. There are three distinguishable layers. The topmost layer consists of Barrule Slates, which form the outcrop of the mountain ridges in the centre of the island. Flanking and underlying these are the quartz-veined Agneash Grits, which are exposed in the south, and also on the eastern slopes of Snaefell and its neighbours. Lowest of all are the Lonan-Niarbyl Flags, which form a coastal strip from Santon to Maughold, reaching inland to Union Mills in the vicinity of Douglas, and also occur between Peel and Niarbyl on the west coast.

The sliding of grit and slate beds relative to one another has resulted in an extensive area of 'crush conglomerate' in the region of Sulby Glen and along the valley of the Sulby river to Ramsey. This was due to the fragmentation of the beds and rearrangement into a form in which pieces of the harder bands are set in a matrix consisting of the crushed softer layers.

If any Silurian of Devonian rocks were deposited on the Isle of Man, they had all been removed by erosion before the Carboniferous period. The next oldest rock strata—from the earlier Carboniferous—occur in three separate sites: the Red Sandstone

Douglas from the air, looking south. The layout of the harbour may be seen, with Victoria Pier nearest to the camera, and King Edward VIII pier parallel (*Manx Technical Publications*)

The central uplands: a typical scene, with signs of the very widespread re-afforestation on the left of the picture (*Manx Press Pictures*)

Peel from the battlements of Peel Castle. The North Quay is in the foreground, the Castle being connected with the South Quay by a causeway (*Manx Press Pictures*)

at Peel; the lowland area round Castletown; and deeper down under the glacial drift beneath the northern plain.

The Peel Sandstone runs in a coastal strip for about 1½ miles north-east of Peel town, with a small extension inland. Together with some conglomerate, the sandstone rests on the upturned edges of the old Cambrian schists below. It is a calcareous stone and contains some fossils characteristic of the Devonian system. The sandstone has been much in use locally as a building stone. There was some carboniferous limestone resting on the sandstone formation, but this has apparently all been quarried and burnt for lime and none of it remains. At Langness, near Castletown, Old Red Conglomerate, similar to that at Peel, runs for about a mile on the inner side of the peninsula and is overlaid on the landward side by later carboniferous rocks.

In this area, the carboniferous rocks consist of limestone and extend from Port St Mary up as far as Santon Burn, along the east coast. The stone has been quarried as much as 3 miles inland. Castletown and its neighbouring villages have been built from this local stone. There is a lime kiln at Billown; formerly there were others at Port St Mary, Scarlett and Ballahot. The limestone layers contained a normal quota of fossils, and on the coast near Castletown ran right to the water's edge. Over the whole south-eastern area, where it is not on the surface, the limestone is covered by alluvial drift and this has given rise to the gentle hills and valleys of the coastal platform.

At Poyllvaish, at the east side of Bay-ny-Carricky, between Castletown and Port St Mary, the stone occurs in thinner flaggy beds; these produce the characteristic local 'black marble' used for fireplaces and mantelpieces—and, according to local tradition, for the original steps of St Paul's Cathedral. These must have been replaced long ago, for it weathers badly and does not endure out of doors.

To the south-east of Castletown, stretching north-west from Scarlett Point to Poyllvaish, there is a strip of igneous rocks,

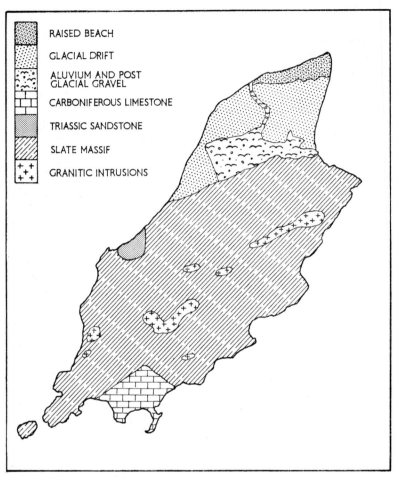

RAISED BEACH

GLACIAL DRIFT

ALUVIUM AND POST
GLACIAL GRAVEL

CARBONIFEROUS LIMESTONE

TRIASSIC SANDSTONE

SLATE MASSIF

GRANITIC INTRUSIONS

Geological

designated as the Carboniferous Volcanic Series. The transition from the undulating Castletown limestone to the typical masses of volcanic agglomerate occurs precisely at Scarlett Point. Scarlett Stack, offshore and isolated at high tide, is a basaltic pile with fused limestone round it. Obviously this is the

20

scene of former volcanic activity, though there is some doubt as to whether the formation is directly due to volcanic eruption or to normal faulting.

Permian and Triassic deposits beneath the northern plain, north of the Ramsey–Kirkmichael line, are covered with 150ft or more of glacial drift material and lie 'in strongly marked unconformability' on the underlying Carboniferous rocks. There is no coal in the island, but there are salt-bearing marls in the Triassic deposits, up to 600ft down, below the Point of Ayre and salt was extracted hydraulically until 1956. The saliferous marls probably rest on St Bees Sandstone, below which there is another thin marl layer, then further sandstone, coarser than the upper one and Permian in origin. Covering these rocks adjoining the Ayres is a considerable area of blown sand. Between this locality and the northern limit of the upland massif lies an intermediate drift platform, including the slight elevations of the Bride Hills. Here also are the Curraghs, a lower area, formerly the beds of lakes which have been more or less adequately drained over the years.

Three successive Ice Ages are thought to have influenced the structure of the Isle of Man. The earliest (Ross) produced the striae on the Manx mountains which were over-ridden by ice. The second glaciation (Würm I) saw the ice rise only to about 1,300ft on the hills, resulting in the thick, smooth blanket of drift which covered the smaller hills, and also caused the valleys of certain rivers to become steeper. The third glaciation (Würm II) affected only the lowland areas. The ice sheets reached the island from the north—from the north-east of Ireland and South-West Scotland, possibly also from Cumbria in England —and boulders from each have been found.

Boulder clays and sand and gravels of varying depths now cover most of the island, except for the higher ground. The most interesting of these are in the chain of low hills running from Jurby to Bride on the northern plain. These form a moraine and were fashioned during a temporary arrest of the recession of the ice sheet, with small valleys formed by the melt water flowing down into what was then a lake on the site of the Curraghs.

At this time, the island probably terminated at the edge of the steep mountain line, running west from Ramsey, with one or two projections northwards. One of the crucial questions concerning the island's earlier development is the date of its separation from the land mass of Great Britain. At one time it was thought there was no connection in the post-glacial period, but it is now believed the land link persisted for a time into the Pleistocene—most recent—period. The Irish Sea is never more than about 140ft deep between the Isle of Man and Lancashire or Cumbria, and much of it is a good deal shallower, so that no enormous geological movement is necessary to establish a bridge.

FLORA AND FAUNA

The natural history of the Isle of Man has been intensively studied. The great botanist John Ray visited the island in 1662 and was the first to record the 'Manx cabbage' near Ramsey. For many years a flourishing Naturalists and Antiquarian Society has kept a close watch on biological developments in the island, the appearance and disappearance of species, and chance visitors among birds.

The varied ecological environments range from different coastal habitats—cliff and rock pools, shingle beaches, salt marshes and sand dunes—to hill and moorland sites and wet areas such as the Curraghs near Ballaugh. There has been an absence of considerable woodland areas in modern times, for clearly the trees were ravaged in the past, whether for fuel or building. However, reafforestation began in 1883 with planting at Archallagan, south-west of St John's and adjacent to the old Cornelly mines. In the next decade 370 acres were planted, the land having been reserved by the Crown under the Disafforestation Act of 1866. Similar schemes were started on South Barrule and at Greeba—the King's Forest. Today there are over twenty different plantations, in all parts of the island. As is usual with such developments, and for economic reasons, the main emphasis has been on conifers, but some hardwoods are being included here and there. The tree plantations, now a considerable feature of the landscape, are under the vigilant care of the Forestry, Mines and Land Board established in 1950.

Plants

There are no special rarities in the plant kingdom in the Isle of Man—no vegetable equivalent to the Manx cat. The peculiarities of form and feature of some plants suggest the production of geographic subspecies due to isolation. The Manx cabbage is probably an example of this.

The limestone area is not sufficiently extensive to produce a lime-loving rock flora and most of it is closely cultivated. There is sand-dune flora on Langness, and all along the northern shores from Kirkmichael to Ramsey. There is also a patch of salt marsh on Langness. Generally speaking the sand-dune flora of the British Isles is well represented.

Mountain plant associations are similar to those of North Wales. There are recent records of two exotic newcomers in the New Zealand willowherb, *Epilobium nerterioides*; also the southern hemisphere moss, *Campylopus introflexus*. No bog myrtle occurs.

The wetlands of the Curraghs are the most interesting area; bog plants flourish and in the drains are bladderwort, frog bit and sundry pond weeds. Considerable clumps of royal fern occur along the drier ridges.

The visitor will note the profusion of primroses in spring; ferns and bluebells in the glens, and, particularly in the south, the ubiquitous fuchsia hedges—the fuchsia has adopted the island as its own. The national flower of the Isle of Man—the Cushag, or ragwort—is found everywhere.

The existing flora seems to support the theory that the land connection with Britain survived the last Ice Age. Investigation of the lower layers of Manx Peat bear this out—the glaciation destroyed the pre-existing flora, but the island was repopulated via the land bridge. The number of plant species to make the crossing in the period during which the land connection persisted would have been limited thus accounting for the present somewhat restricted flora.

Animals

Similar considerations apply to the fauna, though there has been introduction of species by man. For instance, rabbits are thought to have been introduced by the Derbys; then ferrets were introduced to control the rabbits, and some of these have gone wild. Two varieties of hare occur: the mountain hare turns white in winter, similarly to the Irish hare—this may suggest it was introduced; the rival brown hare may be a genuine native. Mice are abundant, both domestic and field types, but there are no squirrels. Nor are there any foxes, though the evidence is that they were the victims of the deafforestation of the Middle Ages. Rats are probably an introduced species; but the pigmy shrew is more likely a native and this tiny animal occurs fairly abundantly in the hedgerows. Three types of bat are found, the most common being the pipistrelle. There are no snakes, toads or newts. Frogs are present, but they are probably an introduced species.

The two characteristic animals are the Manx cat and the Loghtan sheep. The typical Manx cat has long back legs and a complete absence of tail. This produces an unusual gait, which is often compared to that of the rabbit as also is its fur coat. Sometimes Manx cats have a semi-developed tail resembling the scut of a rabbit. Litters of kittens are usually mixed: those with normal tails; 'stumpies', with short tails, and 'rumpies', with no tails. A popular idea has been that the Manx 'rumpy' is in some way a hybrid between the cat and the rabbit, though this is quite out of the question. The Manx cat is a mutation which has been preserved by human selection in the rather restricted genetic environment of the island. The absence of tail may be due to a defect similar to that which causes spina bifida in human beings. The genetics are somewhat complicated as 'stumpies' often produce tail-less kittens.

The Loghtan sheep is remarkable mainly because the rams have a tendency to produce not two, but four horns. It also has characteristic brown wool, fairly thin and with a long staple. It may have been brought to the island by the Scandinavians; it seems to be related to the St Kilda breed and has only persisted through the efforts of a few enthusiasts in recent times. The Manx Museum and National Trust has now taken the matter in hand and is maintaining flocks on the Calf of Man and elsewhere.

The Manx cat has also acquired official protection, in view of the threat posed by immigration in the last two decades, and a government cattery has been established. So both these characteristic creatures can look forward to a protracted and protected existence.

Fish and butterflies

Perch occur, and both salmon and trout are to be found in the rivers. A breeding station was set up at Kirkmichael for brown and rainbow trout as well as salmon and sea trout. Laxey derives its name from the Norse word for salmon.

About sixteen species of butterfly are known.

BIRD LIFE

The Isle of Man is rich in bird life. A recent list noted 66 resident species and a further 29 which breed in the island, while over 250 species in all have been observed. Situated on a main migration route, the Isle of Man receives a large number of visiting birds. Naturally gulls figure prominently: the herring gull, kittiwake and greater black-backed gull are residents, while the lesser black-backed and blackheaded gull both breed. Common, arctic and little terns all breed. Resident water birds include the little grebe, moorhen, heron, oystercatcher, lapwing, ring-necked plover, snipe and curlew; and among sea birds are the fulmar, cormorant and shag, razorbill, guillemot and puffin. The mallard is the only resident duck, though teal and shelduck are known to breed.

Other residents are birds of prey: the sparrowhawk, peregrine and kestrel; and game birds such as red grouse, partridge and pheasant. Five species of dove reside in the island and also the barn owl and long-eared owl. Crows are mostly of the hooded (Irish) variety; ravens are also found, in addition to the predictable rooks, magpies and jackdaws. Skylarks are resident and swallows, martins and swifts breed abundantly. There are four species of tit: great, blue, coal and long-tailed; as well as meadow and rock pipits. All common finches occur, though the bullfinch is a rare visitor.

The Manx shearwater, after becoming extinct in the island, seems to be nesting again in small numbers in the Calf of Man. The redshank is a common winter visitor, but only breeds to a small extent. The coot breeds but is not a resident—the same applies to the stonechat and whinchat, the blackcap, and the warblers: grasshopper, sedge, garden and wood.

There is a variety of habitats in which birds can be observed. The Langness peninsula is excellent for watching waders and wildfowl and for some passerine migrants. Divers and grebes can be seen in Derbyhaven Bay. The Calf of Man is a bird sanctuary under the care of the Manx Museum and National Trust. Apart from the Manx shearwater, a number of sea birds breed here—shag, razorbill, guillemot, puffin, kittiwake and fulmar—as well as the short-eared owl, raven and chough. The sandy heaths of the Ayres provide a contrasting habitat and here the three varieties of tern breed, and others visit. The moorland areas of the island have a sparse bird population compared with the profusion of sea birds inhabiting the considerable stretches of coastal cliff.

CLIMATE AND WEATHER

The Manx climate is broadly similar to that of Ireland, Western Scotland and other places on the temperate western fringes of Europe. Mild winters are the rule; frost and, more especially, snow are rare; summers are cool, rainfall fairly heavy and completely calm days infrequent. In other words, the climate is equable, windy, cloudy and humid.

The island's mountainous nature and its situation near the paths of Atlantic depressions are responsible for very heavy rainfall over much of the central uplands—more than 50in annually—and also for a striking variation in weather and climate between different parts of the island. The prevailing westerly and south-westerly winds from the Atlantic and the Tropics are warm and moist. Their forced ascent over the Manx mountains causes heavy cloud formation, particularly on the East Coast. Winds from SSE through south to SSW have come by a long sea route up St George's Channel and give rise to drizzle. Easterly winds, most common in Spring, arrive from the Lake District or Lancashire, and often provide clear skies but low temperatures. Northerly air streams follow another long sea track down the Northern Channel; they become warmer and more unstable, causing cloud and storms or showers of rain on the west side of the central uplands.

The prevalence of westerly winds is more pronounced in summer, autumn and winter than in spring, when easterlies often produce long spells of cold, dry weather. Of the island's three weather stations, the Point of Ayre records less easterly wind and more periods of calm than the other two at Ronaldsway airport and Douglas; possibly it lies in the lee of the Lake District. Ronaldsway suffers from eddy currents in the region of South Barrule when the wind is north or north-west.

The surrounding sea exercises a moderating influence on temperature. The monthly mean minimum at Douglas of about 40°F (4°C) occurs in February. The maximum monthly mean —in August—is 58·1°F (14°C); the range between minimum and maximum is only 18°.

Summer temperatures in Douglas are significantly lower than those of mainland coastal stations. In the period 1926–50 the highest mean temperature was reached in Douglas in August at 59° F (15° C). Morecambe, Blackpool and Scarborough all had maxima in July at 60·9°, 60·9° and 61·3° F (16° C) respectively. The extreme maximum in Douglas for the period 1923–57 was only 82° F (28° C)

The mean temperature falls to about 50° F (10° C) in October, to 43° F (6° C) in December and to 40–1° F (5° C) in January–February. A slow rise then occurs to 50° F (10° C) in May and 55° F (13° C) in June. Lowest temperatures are reached in January and February, with mean minimums of 36–37° F (3° C) and an extreme January minimum of 19° F (−7° C).

The highest sunshine values are reached in May and June— rather before the highest temperatures are attained. The Manx sunshine record is better than that of places of comparable latitude, if not so good as of those farther south. In the period 1921–50 Douglas had a mean of 4·3 hours of sunshine, daily, compared with Blackpool, 4·1; Scarborough, 3·8; Worthing, 5·0; Jersey, 5·2, and Torquay, 4·7.

Fog occurs most frequently in February and March when sea temperatures are minimal.

In the period 1918–57 Douglas had an average rainfall of 45·1in—rather more than the average for Lancashire and County Dublin. There is considerable variation in this average, however, as the maximum was 57·4in and the minimum only 32·8in. Both Point of Ayre and Ronaldsway have lower averages; about 34in in either case. The wettest period is from October to January.

2   EARLY HISTORY

THERE is no evidence of Palaeolithic man having reached the island. The arrival of man is closely related to the date of its physical separation from the land mass of Britain, estimated to have occurred around 10000–5000BC.

ARCHAEOLOGICAL REMAINS

The earliest archaeological relics are of Mesolithic (ie Middle Stone Age) man, generally thought to have flourished between 8000 and 5000BC, and it is probable that man arrived during this period. Mesolithic man, a primitive food gatherer, characteristically made and used small pieces of flint—known as microliths—which were sharpened by chipping. These were set in bone or else mounted on wooden spears for use in hunting. Such flints have been found in a number of sites, mostly on dry coastal locations and thought to represent temporary encampments of nomadic folk moving from place to place round the island. The sites were usually on light gravelly soils, and vegetation would not have been dense in Mesolithic times. Among them are Glen Wyllin, near Kirkmichael; Ballaqueeney, at Port St Mary; Poyllvaish, between Castletown and Port St Mary;and Santon, at Port Grenaugh on the coast, 6 miles south of Douglas.

Also found in the same locations are flints of a different kind and later period. These are larger, with a marked 'flaking scar' and 'tang' on the body of the implement. Such artefacts strongly resemble those of the Bann Culture, which existed on the banks of the river Bann in Ulster. These were hunting people who used stronger, more effective and altogether less dainty weapons than the first settlers. They must have crossed the sea, as there could not have been any land link with Ireland. Possibly the Bann people flourished until the arrival of Neolithic men, and indeed co-existed with them. There are no traces of dwellings of either Mesolithic people or the Bann settlements.

Neolithic monuments

The Neolithic period was the one in which agriculture began to develop—the cultivation of land and domestication of animals. It also saw the advance of the art of pottery and of the making of polished stone implements. The Neolithic people left considerable relics in the form of megaliths—communal burial sites—of the same general type as those found in many places in Ireland. The new culture probably came from the Eastern Mediterranean, and arrived by sea along the coast of the Iberian Peninsula, France and Britain.

There are a number of striking monuments of the Neolithic period in the island. The most characteristic is at Cashtal-yn-Ard, Ballachrink, on the Maughold peninsula. It contains a row, or gallery, of burial chambers, or cists, running roughly east-west. At the western end is a forecourt, semi-circular in shape, which gives access by a 'portal' of two standing stones to the five burial chambers. These were originally roofed by undressed slabs of stone and would have been covered by an oblong cairn. Inside, unburnt human bones, pottery and flints were found. To the east of the site, which dates from *c* 2000BC, is a burnt area surrounding a small raised mound.

Even larger than Cashtal-yn-Ard, and contemporary with it, is the so-called King Orry's Grave. This is a chambered cairn, 170ft long in all, though a roadway slices through the site. The eastern section is visible by the roadside, showing an arc-shaped forecourt, again with a portal of two standing stones giving access to the burial chamber. The western end also has a forecourt leading to a two-compartment burial chamber.

The third major Megalithic monument is the Meayll Circle near Cregneish, between Port St Mary and Port Erin. It is of unique design, having six pairs of burial chambers arranged in a circular pattern. The roofing slabs and cairn material were removed long ago. When the site was excavated in 1893, burnt human bones were found as well as Neolithic pottery. One piece of potsherd bears the impression of a grain of wheat, suggesting contemporary cultivation of the cereal.

When Ronaldsway Airport was extended during World War II, excavations revealed evidence of another local Neolithic culture. This consisted of a primitive rectangular dwelling, about 24ft by 17ft, with a central hearth; the roof was probably held up by wooden posts. Relics of pottery and tools were found within the site and also bones of domesticated animals. Several polished axe heads were discovered, some of which were made from igneous rock from the Langdale area of the English Lake District. Pottery included wide-mouthed jars with straight sides and round bases, thought to be food-storage vessels. Of special interest are five small, oval, slate plaques, with a design of chevrons and lozenges. Nothing quite like these has been found in the British Isles, but similar, though larger, objects have been discovered in the Iberian Peninsula. This reinforces the idea that the Neolithic cultures travelled round the western seaboard of Europe. There are other examples of 'Ronaldsway Culture' in the Isle of Man.

Bronze Age relics

About 1800BC there was a new wave of immigration by descendants of the Beaker Folk, who had colonised Britain, a century or so previously, from Germany and the Low Countries. The new settlers had mastered the art of working in bronze— this technique too had probably travelled from the Eastern Mediterranean. Stone axes were gradually replaced by the more effective bronze ones. Together with the knowledge of metal working, there came another type of pottery and different burial customs. Smaller cairns marking individual burials took the place of large communal graves for whole families or tribes. Such a cairn may be seen, for example, on the summit of Cronk-ny-Iree-Laa. Bronze Age axes and pottery have been found over a variety of sites, invariably on the coastal plateaux and plains; the greatest concentration being in the northern plain in the neighbourhood of Andreas.

Celtic forts and round houses

A most important event in the island's early history was the arrival, around 200BC, of the Celtic peoples, armed with the techniques for smelting iron. The beginning of the Celtic Iron Age was evidently rather unsettled, judging by the number of forts on hills and promontories. The hill fort on the South Barrule is of main importance, having the remains of two circular ramparts, and the outlines of a number of circular dwellings within the inner rampart. Other hill forts are at Chapel Hill, Balladoole, Arbory; at Cronk Sumark, Sulby; and Castleward, Braddan, on the outskirts of Douglas. Of these, Cronk Sumark—meaning 'Primrose Hill'—is the most prominent; 250ft high, it is a fairly steep and isolated eminence on the edge of the northern plain. There are fortifications on each of its twin peaks—that on the eastern peak may be of later date. Over twenty smaller promontory forts have been noted round the coast—in naturally defensive locations. In some cases—for example, at Clos-ny-Challagh, Malew, and at Cronk-ny-Merriu at Santon—the forts seem to have been occupied at a later period and Norse relics have been excavated inside the fort ramparts.

The most outstanding example of a Manx Celt dwelling is the round house excavated at Ballacaigen. Dr Gerhard Bersu (1889–1964), a distinguished German archaeologist interned on the Isle of Man during World War II, took advantage of his situation to do a vast amount of research. The Ballacaigen site, described as a fort in earlier maps, proved to be the location of two round houses, evidently the residences of Celtic chiefs. The larger one was 90ft in diameter and not more than 12ft high. The roof was dished or slightly domed; it was made of turf taken from land nearby and supported by a timber framework which in turn rested on stout wooden posts of oak, arranged in five concentric rings. These posts, about 8in thick, were made from trees 100–200 years old. The chieftain and his retinue lived around a limestone hearth in the centre of the house, with a wattle screen separating the living quarters from the outer portions, which were used for storage and stabling animals. This round house was tentatively dated between AD100 and 300.

Several other houses of this type have been discovered, notably at Ballanorris, Arbory and at the Braaid, Marown; in some cases stone, as well as wood, appears to have been used in the construction. Their existence—and their relatively undefended character—suggests that there was a fairly long period of peace and settlement. This coincides chronologically with the time of the Pax Romana and—though there is no direct evidence of any Roman sojourn on the island, apart from the finding of a few Roman coins—the presence of Roman galleys on the surrounding seas may well have curbed the activities of any would-be sea raiders on the isles of the western fringe.

Within the ramparts of the promontory fort at Clos-ny-Challagh four round huts with square central hearths were also excavated. Among the finds was a La Tène III brooch of the Colchester type, which is taken to indicate traffic of some sort between East Anglia and the Isle of Man in the first century. Even in prehistoric times there was a certain amount of movement between the island and neighbouring countries. Various relics in the Isle of Man have been compared with corresponding ones in Northern and Southern Ireland, North Wales, North-west England and Southern Scotland. An analysis of about fifty Bronze Age items indicates that the largest proportion, over one-third, came from Northern Ireland; almost as many from North-west England; about one-eighth from

Southern Ireland and Scotland, and about one-tenth from Wales. This may reflect the varying cultural importance of these regions in the development of the island.

EARLY CHRISTIAN CHURCH

Christianity arrived in the western fringe during the Celtic period. The pioneer is believed to be St Ninian (or Trinian) a Scottish missionery who died in AD432. His influence was felt mainly in South-west Scotland and also to a degree in North-east Ireland; and he is believed to have come to the Isle of Man. There is a modern church dedicated to him in Douglas, and an early medieval ruined church, St Trinian's—formerly held by the Priory of St Ninian—at Whithorn in Galloway, Scotland.

There is also a view that St Patrick, the patron saint of Ireland, and his followers, were responsible for the conversion of the Isle of Man. Jocelinus's *Life of Patrick* states that the saint was shipwrecked on the island's west coast in AD444—twelve years after he began his mission in Ireland: 'Finding the people much given to magic, he remained for three years, converting the people to the Christian Faith.' He is said to have landed on St Patrick's Isle (or Holme Patrick) at Peel and to have built a church there. On his departure in 447 he sent his nephew Germanus, or German, as the first Bishop of Man, who in turn established St German's Cathedral Church, also on St Patrick's Isle.

Other Irish missionaries were Mac Cuill or Maughold, to whom an important church was dedicated, and St Brigid of Kildare, whose influence was widespread over all the five countries judging by the churches and villages dedicated in her name; on the Isle of Man itself there is St Brigid's Nunnery, just outside Douglas, and the village of Bride, or Kirk Bride, on the northern plain.

Columba (born 521) had a very considerable influence on the Manx church. While he founded his celebrated monastery

Monas Isle I from a painting in the Manx Museum. The old lighthouse at the end of the Red Pier can be seen on the left of the picture (*Manx Museum*)

Douglas Bay from Douglas Head — possibly the best-loved view in the Isle of Man. In the distance, the peaks of Snaefell and Beinn-y-Phott can be distinguished (*Manx Press Pictures*)

The Isle of Man Railway: a sight that may soon be a thing of the past (*Manx Press Pictures*)

A Douglas horse tram: one of the familiar 'toast racks' which celebrated a centenary in 1975 (*author*)

on Iona, with the object of converting the Picts of Scotland, his school ranged much wider; through two associated monasteries in Ireland its work extended to the Isle of Man, where his followers Ronan and Brendan are commemorated in Kirk Marown and Kirk Braddan.

Keeils

The early Christian Church left many memorials in the island in the form of small primitive chapels, or keeils. Over 180 keeils are known to have existed and vestiges of quite a number remain to this day. They are small, rectangular structures, about 15 × 10ft, in some cases having the remains of an altar at the eastern end. Originally they were primitive erections of sods or wattle and daub, on a stone foundation. Later, from the eighth century, there are examples of stone-faced walls and even of the use of mortar; but more characteristically they had earth walls, faced by dry-stone walling. The architecture is extremely simple: one rectangular chamber with no division into nave and chancel; there may have been a window at the east end and a door at the west. The roofs seem to have been thatched. Even later churches, in early medieval times, were built on much the same pattern. Keeils were widely distributed in the island, though not in the mountainous areas. They were usually sited away from hamlets or villages, and often surrounded by burial grounds. Typical remains may be seen at Spooyt Vane, Kirkmichael; Chapel Hill, Balladoole, and there are three examples in the churchyard at Maughold. It is possible that there was a keeil in every treen—a word of Celtic origin denoting a small land unit of 200–400 acres.

Ogham stones

Also dating from the early Christian period, though considered to be of pagan origin, are the Ogham Stones. Ogham was a form of writing or script of the fourth and fifth centuries, used by the Celts, and particularly widespread in Ireland.

c

It was inscribed on tombstones, usually giving the name of the person buried and of his father. The script consists of straight-line strokes on stone, some being vertical and some at an angle. Five Ogham stones have have been found in the Isle of Man. Four of these are fairly typical, written in Gaelic. The fifth, from Knoc-y-Doonee, Kirk Andreas, has an added Latin inscription in Roman letters and is of great interest because of its bilingual character; it dates from the late fifth or early sixth centuries.

Manx crosses

With the coming of Christianity, crosses replaced Ogham stones as memorials on burial grounds. There are a considerable number of Manx crosses from about AD650 onwards; over 170 carved cross slabs have been found ranging in date from the seventh to twelfth centuries. The earlier Celtic period saw fairly simple forms of the marigold or Maltese cross type; later on, in the ninth century, a different sort appeared, which imitated, in low relief carving, the outline of free standing Celtic High crosses.

Collections of crosses of the Celtic period may be seen in the churchyard at Maughold; at Lonan, near Laxey, and at Onchan—all showing the familiar Celtic interlaced strapwork. The outstanding example of the Celtic cross is the Calf of Man Crucifixion (eighth century); found originally in 1773 and remaining in private hands until 1956, it is now preserved in the Manx Museum. It is remarkable in that Christ appears fully clothed and alive, in a style found otherwise in the art of the Eastern Mediterranean of about the sixth century or later. This type of representation of the Crucifixion probably travelled via the Mediterranean to Ireland, where it also appears, whence it was copied in the Calf of Man example.

Although the arrival of the Celts in the Island may have occurred in a politically turbulent period, the latter centuries of the Celtic era were relatively tranquil and prosperous, no doubt due to the Pax Romana and the civilising influence of Christianity, and traffic expanded between the Isle of Man and its neighbours. A comparison of the island's Celtic crosses with similar ones in surrounding countries shows that at this stage, AD400–800, Southern Ireland seems to have generated one-third of this traffic; Scotland and Wales a quarter each, and North-west England and Northern Ireland one-tenth each. These rough estimates reflect not so much trade as cultural influence between the regions.

THE VIKING ERA

The picture of the island in the Dark Ages is therefore of a peaceful, pastoral society, Christian and Gaelic-speaking. About AD790, however, the situation changed, as the Vikings arrived and steadily spread their influence over the British Isles. The invaders crossed from Denmark and Norway in their long-ships with single square sails, in which they sailed to Iceland and Greenland, and almost certainly as far as America. They were men of violence, who came in the first place to plunder, and specialised in the pillage of abbeys and nunneries. The earliest record of their arrival in the Irish Sea is the sacking in 798 of St Patrick's Isle—but this is generally thought to refer to the island off Skerries, north of Dublin, not the one at Peel. There is little doubt that the Isle of Man came under attack at about the same time, though there are no definite records.

The Vikings, driven from home by food shortages, began to settle in the most fertile areas of the newly conquered territories by the latter part of the ninth century. They settled in Northumbria in 876; Alfred the Great came to terms with them in 886, giving them settlers' rights in the North and parts of the Midlands. From their Irish Sea bases, the Vikings established themselves in North-west England early in the tenth century, and such a strategic island as Man would not have remained unoccupied for long. The invaders took over the fertile districts of the Northern Plain—an area still rich in Norse names.

The same locality contains a number of circular earthen

39

mounds which are probably burial places of early generations of Viking settlers. The mound at Knoc-y-Doonee, a couple of miles south-west of the Point of Ayre, which was excavated in 1927, proved to be a ship burial; the Viking's body was buried in his ship—about 20ft long—with his weapons, horse, dog and domestic tools. A similar grave was excavated at Balladoole, near Castletown; here the ship was 35ft long. Both sites are on hills overlooking the sea. The equipment buried with the warrior was to enable him to hold his own in Valhalla; its variety and ornamentation bears witness to cultural contacts not only with Scandinavia, Ireland and England, but also with central and southern Europe.

Peaceful penetration gradually took the place of aggressive raids, particularly in the islands of the western fringe. The Isle of Man was probably colonised by Norsemen from the area of Dublin, though, owing to its central position, it was easy of access for any of the Viking settlements on surrounding coasts. It can be said that from AD800 to 880 the Norsemen came to plunder, and from 880 to 1000 to settle. The island was under the rule of the earls of Orkney from 990 to 1079 and for over a century it was a convenient pawn in a power struggle between various Norse chiefs, in which Irish rulers played a part from time to time.

KINGDOM OF MAN

A settled period began in 1079 with the reign of Godred Crovan, said to have been the son of Harold the Black of Iceland and to have fought with the Norwegian forces at Stamford Bridge in 1066 against Harold of England. After the defeat he may have fled to the Isle of Man. In 1075 he attacked the island in force; but was repelled on two occasions by the Manx. On the third attempt, in 1079, he came in at Ramsey by night with 600 men and the Manx were surrounded in a bend of the Sulby river where they yielded. Godred treated them generously and ruled the island until 1095. He was a great fighter and, according to legend, a relatively enlightened and respected king, having apparently spent his youth in the island. He is thought to have been the 'King Orry' who has persisted in Manx legend to the present day. He was responsible for the establishment of the Kingdom of Man and the Isles.

The union of the Isle of Man with the Hebrides may have existed administratively at an earlier date. The Hebrides were divided into the Northern Isles (Lewis, Harris, etc)—known as the Northreyjar—and the Southern Isles (the Inner Hebrides, Mull, etc)—Suthreyjar, later corrupted to Sodor—with which Man was classified. Godred initiated the system of government in Man and the Isles, which was centred on the House of Keys, situated in the Isle of Man. When he died in 1095, a period of some turbulence followed, a battle being fought in 1098 by two rival chieftains at a place called Sartwat—probably somewhere near Peel. This may have been a conflict between the mainly Viking north and west parts of the island and the predominantly Celtic south. Victory went to the north, reputedly due to the fierce assistance of the female population.

Godred's two elder sons quarrelled. Lagman, who succeeded his father, put out the eyes of his brother, Harold; then in a fit of penitence, went off on a Crusade, on which he died. The third brother, Olaf, was a young boy and for a time the island suffered under a regent from Dublin, one Dugald, who was eventually driven out. Olaf was accepted as king in 1113 and reigned for forty years, peacefully and wisely, and on good terms with the neighbouring kingdoms. The Cistercian Abbey of St Mary—the so-called Rushen Abbey—was founded at Ballasalla during his reign, the site being granted by the king to the Abbot of Furness in Lancashire.

Olaf met a violent end in 1153, murdered by nephews from Dublin. His son, Godred II, who at the time was in Norway paying homage to the king for his father, returned and rapidly avenged Olaf's death. He then proceeded to occupy Dublin and virtually united the Kingdom of Man with that of Leinster.

Internal quarrels resulted in a rebellion against him, led by his brother-in-law, Somerled, who ruled in Argyll. In 1158 Godred was defeated in a great sea battle off Colonsay, and he was forced to share his kingdom with Somerled. Godred retained Man and the Northern Isles of Lewis and Skye, while Somerled took the Southern Isles, including Mull and Islay. This rather curious arrangement meant that Man was separated from its sister isles to the north by the Southern Hebrides and was 300 miles from its farthest outpost. Godred put himself under vassalage to Henry II of England in self-protection. He was driven off Man once more by Somerled, but returned to reign until 1187. He was buried on Iona.

Godred was succeeded by a bastard son, Reginald I, as Olaf, his rightful heir and legitimate son, was only ten years old. The new king was in the true Viking tradition, a great sea dog and fighter; he is credited with spending three years continuously aboard ship. To appease young Olaf's supporters, he gave him the Kingdom of Lewis. This was not nearly so prosperous or fertile as Man and when Olaf complained Reginald imprisoned him in Scotland. Olaf escaped, raised a fleet, and landed at Ronaldsway in 1224. Civil war raged on the island. Olaf had the support of the northern Manx, Reginald that of the southerners. The decisive battle was fought at Tynwald Hill in 1228 when Reginald was slain. During his reign, he had sworn allegiance to the Pope and paid homage to Henry III of England.

Olaf II gained control of the island on Reginald's death, but could not win back all the other isles. He in his turn pledged vassalage to Henry III and promised to provide fifty ships in the Irish Sea to protect England against the activities of Irish marauders. He was summoned to Norway to explain this to the king, but died before he could set out.

Olaf was succeeded by his teenage son, Harold, who pursued the English connection even more enthusiastically, refusing to recognise the suzerainty of Norway. After being deposed and having his revenues seized by the king of Norway, he again submitted and was reinstated. But when he was knighted by the English King, Harold in turn was summoned to Norway to explain his conduct. This he did so convincingly that he ended by marrying the king's daughter; unfortunately they were drowned when the ship in which they were returning to Man was wrecked off the Shetlands.

A period of confusion ensued for three or four years; finally Magnus, younger brother of Olaf—with the help of John, King of the Isles—became King of Man and the Isles—the last one, as it transpired. Both Scotland and England were casting their eyes upon the Isle of Man and the other isles. Alexander of Scotland took the offensive and defeated Haakon of Norway at the Battle of Largs in 1263. Magnus, in order to keep possession of Man, paid homage to Alexander, though he lost the Isles. He died in 1265; in the following year Scotland and Norway signed a treaty whereby Man and the Isles were handed over to Scotland.

UNDER THE VIKINGS

The effects of the Norse occupation upon the life of the islanders were permanent. Many customs and traditions are directly attributable to Scandinavian influence, though this did not extend markedly to the language. Gaelic was spoken before the Norsemen came, and persisted as the vernacular well into the nineteenth century. It has been suggested that Norse was the language of the ruling classes, the Viking aristocracy and land-owners. Most of the settlers were probably male, relatively few women making the long sea voyage; wives would therefore have been sought among the Gaelic-speaking natives, and children would have picked up the Gaelic from their mothers. It is also possible that there was considerable immigration into Man from the surrounding Gaelic-speaking countries in the post-Scandinavian period. However, a considerable number of Norse place names and surnames survive in the island.

Norse houses and crosses

The Norsemen lived in long, narrow dwellings, about 35 × 14ft, with low walls of stones and earth, and a steep roof of turf, straw and rushes. They had central hearths with a hole in the roof to let the smoke out. On each side of a central aisle there were raised platforms or sleeping benches along the long walls. In settlements, the landowner and his retinue lived in separate houses set in squares; even the rooms—such as the kitchen or dining room—might each be a separate building. Large family units were the rule, with sons and even daughters remaining in residence after marriage and raising their families in the same place.

Remains of a number of such houses have been found in the island—some in coastal promontory forts of an earlier date, as at Cronk-ny-Merriu, Santon, or even on the same site as a Celtic round house, as at the Braaid, Marown. This latter site shows evidence of three successive houses on one farmstead, suggesting occupation over several centuries from the Celtic into the Norse period.

The Viking invaders were evidently converted to Christianity quite quickly—probably by intermarriage—for within a generation or so they were erecting stone carved cross slabs as grave monuments. This custom was a direct continuation of Celtic practice, but the character of the carvings on the crosses changed, introducing figures and animals and even scenes from pagan Norse mythology—in particular, representations of Sigurd the Volsung, examples of which can be seen in several places on the island. In Andreas and Malew especially there are crosses on which Sigurd is shown roasting the dragon's head and sucking his fingers. Many of the crosses bear runic inscriptions, indicating the person to whom the cross is dedicated or, in some cases, the identity of the sculptor who carved it. Crosses in Andreas and in Michael, for example, are carved by Gaut, presumably the same person.

Land divisions

The Isle of Man was—and is to this day—divided into six sections, or sheadings; all, except Garff, being composed of three parishes. On the west side, from south to north, are:

Glenfaba with the parishes of Patrick, German and Marown
Michael with the parishes of Michael, Ballaugh and Jurby
Ayre with the parishes of Lezayre, Bride and Andreas

And on the east side, from south to north:

Rushen with the parishes of Malew, Arbory and Rushen
Middle with the parishes of Braddan, Onchan and Santon
Garff with the parishes of Maughold and Lonan

The precise meaning of the word 'sheading' is not clear. The Oxford English Dictionary now accepts that it comes from the Middle English 'scheding' meaning a division—also found in the word 'watershed'. On this basis it might well have been introduced by the Stanleys in the fifteenth century. Others maintain that it means a sixth part and is either a Celtic or Norse term. A more romantic but quite plausible explanation is that it is derived from *skeid-thing*, meaning an assembly or community (*thing*) represented by a ship or ships. This supposedly dates back to the time when each *skeid-thing* was responsible for providing a definite number of ships, probably four, for communal defence of the island.

It may well be that the boundaries of the sheadings correspond to some more ancient communal divisions, but under Scandinavian rule they were made more definite. Each sheading had its own *thing*—a sort of miniature Tynwald dealing with questions of revenue and land ownership.

The parishes have long been basic units in the organisation of civil life and even of military affairs. The rank of Captain of the Parish still exists; now elected by the citizens of the parish, he was originally in charge of the raising of militia from within his own area. Although the name did not come into use till the medieval period, no doubt the function was exercised from an earlier date. There were probably only sixteen parishes originally, Santon and Marown being separated at a later time. Each parish had a church as its focal point, and most parishes are prefixed 'Kirk' from the Norse *kirkja*, church.

Treens are much smaller land units, usually 200–400 acres in extent, and are sub-divided into quarterlands. These four subsections correspond roughly to modern farm units, though some have been further divided. The quarterlands are usually prefixed with 'Balla', as in Ballaskelly, Ballacowle and Ballacree in Kirk Bride parish. The names of treens vary with the district; in Ayre sheading, for example, there are nineteen Norse names and fifteen Gaelic. It has been suggested that the word 'treen' implies that it was a third part of some larger unit, but this conflicts with its sub-division into four, not three, parts. Another view is that 'treen' is derived from the Irish *triunga*, or ounceland used in the Hebrides. There is general agreement that treens and quarterlands represent traditional land divisions, with a very long history behind them, probably predating the Scandinavian occupation.

THIRTEENTH–FOURTEENTH CENTURIES

The assumption of control of the island by Alexander of Scotland in 1266 ushered in a rather turbulent period during which England and Scotland contested with one another for its possession. Manx chieftains did not take kindly to Scottish sovereignty, and Alexander came to terms, promising 'not to go to Mann for a space of time'. He sent officials in 1275 and this provoked a rebellion under Godred, son of King Magnus. A Scottish fleet landed at Ronaldsway and defeated the Manx on land; Godred was slain and Godred Crovan's line came to an end.

Alexander's granddaughter, Margaret—the 'Maid of Norway' who had succeeded him on the throne—died in 1290.

Edward I of England was asked to adjudicate between the various claimants to the Scottish Crown and decided in favour of John Balliol. The new ruler took possession of Man, but the English King made it clear that he expected Balliol to acknowledge his sovereignty over both Scotland and the Isle of Man. Balliol rebelled against this, but was defeated by Edward and the island passed into English hands. The Bishop of Durham, a most warlike Christian, was appointed as Governor. England continued in control and in 1311 Edward II appointed the notorious Piers Gaveston as Lord of Man, though his rule was short, as he was executed after provoking the English court nobles into rebellion.

In 1313 Robert the Bruce—as a claimant to the Scottish throne—also claimed the Lordship of Man. He besieged and overthrew the English garrison at Castle Rushen, which was damaged in the struggle, and handed over the Lordship to his supporter, the Earl of Moray. The Isle of Man was now bound to provide one ship of twenty-six oars from each sheading for the Scottish fleet.

With Bruce's death in 1329, Edward III granted the island to Sir William Montacute—later Earl of Salisbury—and his heirs in perpetuity, and from this time the Lords of Man were all English. Montacute sold his title in 1392 to the Earl of Wiltshire, who was executed by Henry IV, whereupon it was granted to the Earl of Northumberland. He in his turn was accused of treason and in 1405 the Lordship was granted to Sir John Stanley, his heirs and assigns 'with its castles and royalties not exceeding £400 a year and the patronage of the see'. In return the Lord was to render 'two falcons on paying homage and two falcons to all future Kings of England on the day of their coronation'.

Buildings of the period

It seems that life on the island had reached a low ebb at this time, as a result of 140 years of unsettled government and plunder by raiders. Nevertheless—or perhaps for this reason—several of the island's most prominent buildings date from this period. Among them are Peel Castle, though parts of the structure, including the Round Tower and St German's Cathedral are of earlier date; Castle Rushen—again an earlier building—existed on the same spot; Maughold parish church; Lonan Old Church; St Trinian's, near Crosby, and, with later additions, Bishopscourt, the official residence of the Bishops of Sodor and Man.

Three Legs symbol

The fourteenth-century Pillar Cross in Maughold churchyard is of great interest, being the earliest example of the Three Legs of Man. This symbol—which, along with the tail-less cat, is the island's most widely known feature—is probably very ancient, as it is said to have been seen on a Greek vase of 500–600 BC. Certainly it found its way into Sicily and was used in coinage in the fourth century BC. It is generally considered to have derived from the swastika which also appears on the Isle of Man in some Scandinavian crosses. There is no evidence of continuity between its use in Sicily and Man. It is not known in Sicily in medieval times; nor does it appear in Man until at least the thirteenth century. Another view traces its origin to the tenth-century Norse-Irish kings of Dublin and northern England who used a triple knot on their coins—the Manx Norse kings were of the same dynasty. The three legs symbol is said to have been used by Henry de Bello Monte, Lord of Man in 1310, and by the Earl of Moray, Bruce's henchman, in 1313. It was undoubtedly in use as the arms of the island in the fourteenth century. Apart from the Maughold cross, it appears in a seal used by Sir William Scrope, Lord of Man in 1395. The Latin motto, which is the Manx national motto, *Quocunque Jeceris Stabit* (Wherever you throw it, it stands) dates from much later (see plate 15).

48

3   THE RULE OF THE STANLEYS

BETWEEN 1405 and 1736, twelve Stanleys ruled as Lords of Man. The first, Sir John Stanley (I), never visited the island; on his death in 1414 he was succeeded by his son, also John, who took more interest in his kingdom—until 1504 the Stanleys were known as 'kings of Man'. John Stanley (II) found that the Bishop and the Abbot of Rushen were the chief 'barons' of the island, controlling the Church's extensive lands, and Stanley proceeded to curb their power. He forbade them to give sanctuary to any of his tenants who had commited crimes; if they did so, their property would be forfeit. They were also commanded to render homage to the king of Mann at Tynwald—the 'barons' were so called because they paid no rent for their lands, but did homage for it instead. However, three of the insular barons—the Prior of Whithorn in Galloway, the Abbot of Furness in Lancashire and the Prior of St Bees in Cumberland (all English or Scottish abbeys)—failed to do so and were deprived of their lands in consequence.

Stanley had to face two revolts against his governors, which he repressed; he ordered that in future any offence against his appointed governor would be regarded as treason. He codified the laws and started the practice of keeping records of legal cases; he also defined the rights and duties of the people, the Church and the king. A historic law was passed in 1429, laying down that disputes should in future be decided peaceably; trial by contest was thereby abolished. Within the limits of the prevailing despotism of the time, John Stanley (II) seems to have

49

been an enlightened and wise ruler who instituted many valuable reforms.

In the next 200 years few of the Stanleys even visited the Isle of Man. Thomas Stanley (II), who reigned from 1460 to 1504, was created Earl of Derby, and his son, Thomas (III)—besides renouncing the title of 'king' in favour of 'lord'—also had occasion to visit the island to cope with some civil disturbances, the story of which is preserved in an old ballad.

FEUDAL SOCIETY

The Manx people lived in a typical feudal environment at this period. They were tenants who paid their Lord their rent in kind—with corn, sheep, cattle or by their labour. Food had to be supplied to soldiers in garrison at the castles of Peel and Rushen. Taxes were also payable—for the right to fish for herring, the import and export of goods, and the grinding of corn in the Lord's mills. This regulation led to a certain amount of clandestine domestic milling which was put down firmly by authority when it was discovered. No tenant was allowed to leave the island without written licence; if he did so, he might be treated as a felon and his goods seized. Men between twenty and sixty years of age were forced to train as militiamen in the art of the bow and arrow, and the sword and buckler. Every man was also compelled to stand his duty of keeping 'watch and ward' both day and night at various stations round the coast to guard against invasion from the sea.

THE REFORMATION

Little is known about the Reformation in the Isle of Man, except that it was slower to develop than in England and was not accompanied by any excesses. The monasteries were suppressed; property belonging to the Nunnery in Douglas, to Rushen Abbey and to the Friary at Bemaken in Arbory was seized by the Crown and the buildings were abandoned. The third Earl of Derby, who was Lord from 1521 to 1572, was himself a Catholic and this may have helped to mitigate any dire consequences of the great religious change. On the death of the fifth Earl in 1594, the Lordship was in dispute; it was held by the Crown until 1610 when William the sixth Earl resumed control.

THE CIVIL WAR

In 1627 the Lordship passed to William's son, James, on his twenty-first birthday. He was in power till 1651, spanning the troubled period of the Civil War, and was known as 'Y Stanlagh Moar'—the Great Stanley. He broke with tradition by appointing a Manxman as governor. Edward Christian, son of the vicar of Maughold, was a considerable adventurer and businessman, constantly in and out of the Lord's favour. During the Civil War he was in charge of the militia and was imprisoned for inciting them to rebellion—feelings were running high among the people, particularly on the payment of tithes. Stanley had the tithes reduced, but introduced a system of land tenure whereby no family could lay claim to a piece of land for more than three generations. He thus deprived tenants of their privilege of passing it on indefinitely from father to son, even though it was held only on an annual basis. Stanley also fortified the island—his fort at Derbyhaven still stands. He was captured by the Parliamentarians at the battle of Worcester and executed at Bolton.

During his absence from the island, William Christian, a distant cousin of Edward and son of a deemster (a justice), organised a popular rising, and Parliament eventually took control. Christian was dismissed from his post as receiver-general following the discovery of certain irregularities and he left to live in Lancashire in 1659. At the Restoration, the eighth Earl of Derby pursued Christian—then in prison for debt in London—and had him executed extremely summarily, while an appeal on a question of legality was still pending. Eventually the appeal succeeded, Christian's name was cleared posthumously and his estates restored. Known as Brown Haired William or Illiam Dhone, he occupies a unique place as a national hero since he obviously reflected an underlying discontent.

THE RESTORATION

The island experienced no great change in condition under the Commonwealth or at the Restoration. The Church, however, did increase its power and tighten its discipline, largely due to the Bishop, Isaac Barrow. He also used his authority as governor of the island to improve the lot of the Manx people—his clergy being then so impoverished that they were forced into other occupations, even keeping alehouses. He bought back the tithes which had been lost to the Lord at the Reformation; he established schools, and bought two farms near Castletown, the rents to be used for the support of a school. Out of this, in 1830, King William's College, the well-known public school at Castletown developed.

Smuggling

Smuggling was giving a great impetus to Manx trade at this time and this had far-reaching consequences for the island. The English Navigation Acts specified that goods could only be imported into England in ships built and manned by Englishmen. This was hardly satisfactory for a race of seafarers like the Manx, so they resorted to smuggling activities. Tea, tobacco, silks, wines and spirits from overseas—particularly France, Spain and Scandinavia—were imported into the Isle of Man, and Manx duties, which were light, were paid on them. They were then conveyed, clandestinely, to the English coast and landed, without payment of excise, in small boats specially designed to outsail and elude the revenue cutters.

After the Act of Union with Scotland in 1701, the English Parliament considered making Manx duties equal to those of

A coach of the Snaefell Mountain Railway (*Manx Press Pictures*)

The Point of Ayre lighthouse, standing on the tip of the northern plain; the flatness of the district striking by contrast with the rest of the island (*Isle of Man Tourist Board*)

Ronaldsway Airport where about one third of the visitors get their first sight of the island (*Isle of Man Tourist Board*)

The Douglas passenger terminal, built in 1965, offers shelter to those waiting to embark. It also houses the Harbour Board, and is used occasionally for social functions in winter (*Manx Press Pictures*)

Britain, but the House of Keys negotiated an agreement whereby Parliament would allow certain Manx products to be imported duty free and the Keys would undertake that all imports of foreign goods from the Isle of Man to Britain would be subject to full duty. Tynwald passed an act to this effect, but Parliament did not fulfil its part of the bargain and smuggling recommenced. In consequence of this, Parliament passed a bill, the Imperial Act of 1726, against smuggling, which was eventually to enable the government to purchase the sovereign rights of the Isle of Man.

Land tenure

During the reign of William, ninth Earl of Derby, the question of land tenure came to a head. Despite the introduction of leases imposed by the seventh Earl, most people clung to the old system of tenure, disregarding warnings that under the old system they could be put out at any time, whereas the lease guaranteed tenure for two or three generations. The eighth Earl reiterated his right to dispossess any tenant of his land. Uncertainty as to landowners' rights, and some bad harvests, led to a number of farms becoming empty. After the death of the ninth Earl, his successor, John—the tenth Earl and last of the Stanley rulers of Man—along with Bishop Wilson and three members of the Keys, made an Act of Settlement. This secured tenants in possession of their farms in perpetuity, subject to payment of a yearly rent—the Lord's Rent—which was fixed at a sum never to be altered. This Act has been called the Manx Magna Carta; it virtually turned the tenants into landowners possessing the rights of sale and inheritance, subject to the Lord's Rent.

While this ended the feudal system to all intents and purposes, the civil liberties of the people were still limited. They might be fined, punished and imprisoned without a jury trial; and the governor or his agents were able to extort money. The Keys, formerly a self-electing, self-perpetuating body, became subject to selection by the governor after the Restoration, so that he could dismiss the House if it did not comply with his wishes.

BISHOP WILSON

A redoubtable figure appeared on the Manx scene in 1698. Thomas Wilson, born in 1663, was appointed Bishop of Sodor and Mann at the age of thirty-four and served—or ruled—in this capacity for fifty-seven years.

> He came to the Isle of Man when the people were in great distress, owing to the troubles about land, and when their hitherto simple and uneventful lives were beginning to be affected by the exciting and demoralizing trade of smuggling. They were therefore disposed to rebel against the discipline of the Church; and yet the Bishop was able for nearly 40 years to prevent most of them from rebelling.

Bishop Wilson is said to have given at least one-fifth of his income to pious uses; when a famine occurred in 1739 not only did he give away grain from his own farms but he also purchased cargoes for distribution to the needy. He refused to indulge in pluralism—that is, holding more than one ecclesiastical living at a time, which was then a common practice; nor could he be tempted away from the Isle of Man by the prospect of a richer See elsewhere. He strove to improve the pay and living conditions of his clergy, and rebuilt many of the Manx churches which he found in ruins. He assisted in the Act of Settlement and was behind the Keys in their efforts at emancipation. Above all, he showed interest in the islanders' welfare, especially in encouraging agriculture and fishery. He also appointed full-time teachers, established grammar schools in the towns and provided a library in every parish. He took steps—the first steps—towards providing literature in the Manx language, which was then the vernacular, while insisting that children be taught to read in English.

Ecclesiastical courts

Bishop Wilson was a staunch upholder of Church rights and privileges. A conflict with the civil power arose when the governor refused to let his soldiers, who acted as policemen, arrest persons sentenced at ecclesiastical courts by the vicars-general and imprison them in the Crypt under St German's Cathedral. The governor declined to recognise the right of ecclesiastical courts to punish members of the castle households and garrisons; he also allowed people sentenced by the Church to appeal to civil courts. The crisis point was reached in 1722 when the bishop passed a sentence on the governor's wife for slandering another lady, and ordered her to acknowledge her offence in public. The governor commanded these and other proceedings to be cancelled, but the bishop and the vicars-general refused. Nor would they pay the heavy fines imposed, and were eventually imprisoned in Castle Rushen. Following an appeal to the Privy Council, they were released after nine weeks. The result of the appeal, which took two years to reach, did not support ecclesiastical privilege, though it was in some respects favourable to the bishop.

This did not end 'presentments' to the courts of the Church; in 1790 Thomas Haman was 'presented' for swearing by his conscience and making use of the word 'divel' in his common talk. At another presentment Thomas Caine was summoned 'for not attending Divine Service on the Sabbath Day and for cursing Elizabeth Callister with the words "Plague upon thee"'. People did not usually appear in court and were fined two shillings and sixpence as a rule for 'contempt' and ordered to be admonished by the pastor for their offence. These presentments were much reduced and imprisonment less in evidence after the appeal to the Privy Council. Church and state reached a more stable relationship.

By an enactment of James I, the Lordship of Man passed to a descendant of the seventh Earl of Derby's third daughter—James the second Duke of Atholl. When the new Lord attended his first Tynwald, he was all the more welcome because of the islanders' disenchantment with the rule of the Stanleys. He presided over the 1737 Bill of Rights which ensured the right of all to trial by jury. The Duke died in 1764 and the title passed to his daughter, Charlotte, and her husband, John, who were the last Lord and Lady of Man.

Trade and taxation

Smuggling from the Isle of Man was still a very serious matter for England and the trade was said to be worth a third of a million pounds annually. Furthermore, as goods for smuggling into England were imported legally into the island, and harbour dues were payable, the Lord of Man actually gained financially from the trade. Manx people were widely implicated in smuggling and probably a good deal of economic growth resulted from it. It was therefore decided that the sovereignty of Man must pass back to the King of England and he should appoint officers to collect Manx customs duties. This was seen by the Manx as taxation without representation—in a speech, Edmund Burke compared the island with North America in this respect.

The Duke of Atholl, when approached on the disposal of his rights, refused to hurry his decision on the grounds that he had only recently succeeded to the title. Parliament began to take measures to speed up the proceedings, including a bill to permit Britain to stop and search all boats entering or leaving the island, and to allow offences committed in Man to be tried in British or Irish courts. Eventually a sum of £70,000 was agreed between the duke and parliament, to include the sovereignty of the isle and the collection of customs duties. The duke retained certain manorial rights, such as the ownership of minerals, and the appointment of the bishop and many of the clergy.

Life was made more difficult now because parliament would only permit dutiable goods to reach Man after importation into Britain; later these goods were only permitted in small quantities, conferring some degree of monopoly status on the fortunate few licensed to import them. The Manx people were not favourably impressed by the new arrangement; many had large stocks of dutiable goods on their hands with no prospect of profit. The Keys sent an emissary to Westminster to plead for them, but he received cavalier treatment.

The British government now paid the cost of administration and any surplus from taxation in the Isle of Man was supposed to be spent for the islanders' benefit. Such was not the case, however, and the excess was swallowed up by the British exchequer.

The third Duke of Atholl died in 1774, and the fourth Duke asked for a new financial agreement on the grounds that the original was less than just to him. The Keys resisted this, and abolished the unpopular herring tax and also the turf tax; they also demanded the curtailment of his manorial rights; new roads and bridges, and the draining of the Northern Curraghs. The duke complained to parliament about the conduct of the Keys.

In 1793 he was made governor of the island, his post carrying a good deal of patronage with it, by which he contrived to oblige a number of friends and relatives. He built Castle Mona, near the foreshore in Douglas, as his official residence. He did carry out some popular policies, including the exemption of Manx seamen from the press gang. He also posed as the friend of the people against the Keys which, he said, 'were no more representative of the people of Mann than of the people of Peru'. On the other hand, his nephew, George Murray, was appointed bishop and promptly demanded a tithe of 12 shillings an acre on potatoes; this led to riots and the Palace at Bishopscourt was threatened by an angry mob. Shortly after this, in 1828, the duke sold his remaining rights for £417,000 and left the island for good; this sum was reimbursed out of the island revenue by 1866.

The British government now had control of the island finances and for a period exploited the position to the disadvantage of the Manx; much needed construction works on harbours, roads, and so on were neglected. It was not until 1866, under the enlightened governorship of Lord Loch, that the Isle of Man came to a more satisfactory arrangement with the British exchequer.

THE CHURCH

The leading part played by the heads of the Church on the island will already be evident. After Bishops Barrow and Wilson came Bishop Hildesley, who carried through the translation of the Bible into Manx. He was not a strict disciplinarian and it may be that the decay of the clergy in the eighteenth century was responsible for the success of Wesleyan Methodism. This was first introduced by the 'weeping prophet', John Murlin, in 1758. Wesley himself came to Man in 1777 and 1781; he was favourably impressed with the Manx: 'loving and simple hearted, for they have but six Papists and no Dissenters'. In 1775 there were only fifty-three Methodists, but by 1848 there were 3,050, and fifty-four chapels on the island.

The Roman Catholic population—never as scanty as Wesley believed!—had no place of worship until 1813. Catholic families —especially those from Northern Ireland—brought their chaplains with them to the island. The first Catholic Church was St Brigid's on the old Douglas–Castletown road.

On the island today the Church of England has its Bishop of Sodor and Man; an archdeacon and four canons—St Columba, St German, St Maughold and St Patrick, and twenty-nine parishes. The Roman Catholics have eight churches, the Methodists thirty-two and the United Reformed Church three. Also represented are Baptists, Independent Methodists, Jehovah's Witnesses, Spiritualists and the Salvation Army.

The Church of England is still established and the bishop is present as of right at the sittings of Tynwald. His traditional residence at Bishopscourt is being presented to the nation.

4   THE INDEPENDENT ISLE?

CONSTITUTIONAL questions have always been prominent in Manx history and are no less so at the present time. Manxmen are proud of their long tradition of 'representative government' and jealous of their national identity, or 'Manxness'. On the whole they tend to identify more closely with the Nordic strain in their ancestry, which has given them their government and their traditional way of life, than with the Celtic strain, which has bequeathed them chiefly a language no longer in everyday use.

ORIGINS OF ISLAND GOVERNMENT

The origin of Manx representative government cannot be accurately fixed in time. Assuming that Celtic society was tribal and based on rule by chiefs, then any wider governing assembly was first introduced by the Norsemen, sometime after AD800.

As was their custom, the Vikings set up a *Thing*—an annual or biannual assembly of the freemen of the community at which new laws would be read and agreed, disputes settled and other business transacted. The *Thing* would be held in an open space (*Völlr*) and the meeting known as *Thingvöllr*. The essential features of a *Thingvöllr* are a low hill, joined by a pathway on the east to a courthouse, which was also a place of some religious significance; all was enclosed, or fenced, and surrounded by green.

The site chosen was Tynwald Hill, near St John's, rather to

the west of the centre of the island. This terraced mound was probably a burial place of the Bronze Age where pagan assemblies were held long before the Vikings arrived. Excavations show that there were Viking burials in the vicinity of the present-day Chapel of St John (this dates from 1849, but there are references to much earlier structures) and suggest the existence of a temple dedicated to Thor, where sacrifices would have been carried out before the king attended the court.

On assembly days, rushes were strewn on the path—a tribute to the ancient God, Mannanan Beg MacLir, from whom the Isle of Man is supposed to derive its name. Discussions would be held on the business of the day and when decisions had been taken, the whole company moved in procession to the hall. There the Lawman would pronounce judgement on offenders waiting on the north side of the mound; recite the old laws, and announce any proposed new ones for the approval of the assembly. At this time, there were no written laws and the oral recitation by the Lawman—the so-called Breast Law—was most important. Punishments were summary. Tradition associates the slopes of nearby Slieau Whallian with executions in which the criminal was rolled down in a spiked barrel. The day then finished with feasting.

The word *Thingvöllr* was modified in the course of time to 'Tynwald' in the Isle of Man, and to 'Thingwall' and 'Dingwall' in other parts of the United Kingdom. The Icelandic parliament, or Althing, was established in AD930 and it is known that Iceland was first colonised by Norsemen from Ireland, the Isle of Man and the Hebrides. It is therefore assumed by Manxmen, and not unreasonably, that a *Thing* was set up on their island at an earlier date than in Iceland—probably in the latter half of the ninth century.

The custom was for assemblies to take place at the summer soltice. The early Christians adopted this midsummer celebration, naming it after John the Baptist—24 June being his saint's day. After the change of calendar in the 1780s, this was moved on eleven days to 5 July, on which date the Midsummer Assembly is still held.

Sessions of Tynwald had four sorts of participants. Firstly there was the king, ruler or lord, whose assent was necessary for any new legislation or verdict. He was advised on legal points by two deemsters; these were, and are still, the chief justices of the island. The two may have originally represented the north and south of Man but are now known as First and Second Deemster, without geographical qualification. The Lord was also advised by his chief officials, or council. Tynwald's fourth element was the assembly of Keys, originally the 'worthiest men in the Island'; it was the indispensable presence of these men which permits the use of the word 'representative' for the Tynwald gathering.

'Keys' was thought to be an anglicisation of the words 'kiare-as-feed' which is the Manx for twenty-four. However, in a Statute Book of 1417, the Keys are called *Claves Manniae et Claves Legis*—the keys of Man and keys of the law: the men who would unlock, or solve, the mysteries of the law. Colloquially they were no doubt known as the 'kiare-as-feed' so long as Manx was the vernacular. It has also been suggested that another derivation is possible—from a Scandinavian word *kjosa* meaning 'chosen'; probably the true explanation lies between the first two.

Tynwald has not administered summary justice since 1755 when a man from Ballaugh had his body and goods forfeit to the Lord of Man (at that time the Duke of Atholl) for sheep stealing. Today it is an occasion of some considerable formality, though none the less significant. The central role is now played, not by the Norse king of Man, but by the lieutenant governor—in former times the governor—as representative of the British Monarch who, since the Revestment of 1765, is Lord of Man. He arrives from Douglas by motor car and with a police escort rather than from Castle Rushen with train of a hundred horse. He is received by a guard of honour, and a religious service is held in the Chapel of St John, after which there is a procession to Tynwald Hill. The first man in the procession is the sword bearer, holding the thirteenth-century sword of state with point upward; then comes the lieutenant governor with his small entourage; then the Bishop of Sodor and Man, followed by the Deemsters, the Legislative Council and the Keys.

The governor sits on the summit of the hill, facing east, with the legislative council around him. The second tier of the terraced hill is occupied by the Keys, headed by their speaker. The third platform is occupied by the high bailiff, vicar-general, heads of local authorities, clergy and Free Church ministers. On the fourth level are captains of parishes—formerly commanders of militia companies. The coroners stand at the foot of the Hill; and the coroner of Glenfaba Sheading, in which Tynwald Hill stands, opens the proceedings by 'fencing the court'. This involves reading a proclamation in which all those assembled are admonished not to quarrel, brawl or make any disturbance.

New laws which have been passed during the year are then promulgated. At one time no law was valid until it had been read on Tynwald Hill, but this practice was abandoned during World War I. The royal assent now completes the passage of any new bill; reading on Tynwald is a formality. Laws used to be read in full, but now only a summary is given, the First Deemster reading in English and the Second Deemster following in Manx. The First Deemster then calls for cheers for the Queen and the assembly returns to the Chapel where a formal meeting of Tynwald is held to conclude the day's events.

The form of the traditional Tynwald—the joint assemblies of the house of Keys and the legislative council—is thus maintained, but the functions of the participants have changed considerably and an understanding of the present governmental relations of the Isle of Man necessitates some review of their history.

THE ISLE OF MAN

The Keys

There are twenty-four Keys. The reason for this precise number is by no means clear. It has been explained by reference to the early organisation of the Norse kingdom of Man and the Isles. This was divided into Man on the one hand and, on the other, the four divisions of the Hebrides—northern: Lewis group and Skye group; southern: Mull group and Jura group. Man, being the wealthiest island and capital, appointed sixteen Keys, and the four groups four each, or sixteen in all; this made a grand total of thirty-two Keys meeting each year at Tynwald Hill. When Somerled defeated Godred II in 1156, he annexed the southern group, of Mull and Jura, lying south of Ardnamurchan Point. This reduced the number of Hebridean Keys to eight and the total at Tynwald to twenty-four. After the Battle of Largs and the cession of the Isles to Scotland in 1266, the eight Keys from the outer Isles no longer appeared in Man, but their places were maintained. It is probable, though not proven, that originally one Key was elected from each of the sixteen parishes of the Isle of Man. This arrangement was upset when the number of Keys was changed to twenty-four, and the six sheadings became the basis of representation.

The Keys at this time acted mainly as a kind of jury—helping the deemsters in cases of doubt or difficulty; they were the supreme court of appeal until the Act of 1866 abolished this function. They were also a self-elected and self-perpetuating body—chosen from the ranks of 'freeholders'. In the sixteenth and seventeenth centuries the Keys took a greater part in the making of legislation, though not without opposition from the Stanleys, then the Lords of Man. Nevertheless all legislation required the approval of the Lord, though not of the English sovereign. The Keys lost some authority after the Restoration of 1660 when the eighth Earl of Derby removed some seven members of the House on suspicion of being favourable to Illiam Dhone; and he challenged them again in 1668 over a

66

verdict which seemed to question his ownership of the land. A series of squabbles about customs duties followed and it was not till 1737 that the Keys established the principle that taxation could not be altered without their consent.

More control of island affairs

Following the Isle of Man Purchase Act of 1765, generally referred to as the Revestment Act, the constitutional position was that the island had its own legislature, but all the insular receipts in the way of customs and other dues and taxes were paid into the British exchequer, and the expenses of the island were defrayed partly by charges on the consolidated fund and partly from money voted in supply. There followed a period of administrative stagnation and indifferent executive control with a shortage of money for government and therefore little in the way of public works. Discontent was widespread and it was to appease this that the fourth Duke of Atholl was appointed governor in 1793. Social unrest was by no means quelled in the next fifty years, which saw the disruption of the French revolutionary wars, the Napoleonic campaigns and the Continental disturbances of 1830. The Keys were still a self-elected body, based on a system of nomination and ultimate selection by the governor, and pressure developed for a more popular method of election.

Finally, in 1866, the Isle of Man Customs, Harbours and Public Purposes Act was passed at Westminster. This separated Manx revenues from those of the United Kingdom and gave Tynwald limited control over insular expenditure, subject to the approval of the Treasury in London and to the veto of the governor. The sum of £10,000 was to be paid annually into the United Kingdom exchequer from Manx customs revenue to cover the cost of government in respect of law courts, police and salaries of the governor and his staff. The parliamentary provisions which made available finance for public works in the island were linked with the

67

institution of a popularly elected House of Keys, by the same electoral system as for the British Parliament. The last 100 years have witnessed a general tendency for Tynwald to be given more and more control of Manx affairs.

CUSTOMS REVENUE

The Isle of Man Customs Act of 1887 gave Tynwald power to impose, alter or abolish customs duties, subject to confirmation by act of parliament. The acts of 1866 and 1887, strictly interpreted, meant that Tynwald would have no power to levy taxes or spend money without the consent of the Westminster parliament, but in practice a system grew up in which the annual budget, presented by the lieutenant governor—as the governor was now known—was able to anticipate the year's revenues and expenditure, and to spend money in the year in which it was earned. As duties increased and more and more tourists came to the island, the collecting procedure for Manx customs needed rationalising.

The Common Purse

The Common Purse arrangement has been in force since 1894; under this, differences in customs duties between the Isle of Man and the United Kingdom were virtually eliminated. The British Commissioners of Customs and Excise administer the insular customs, collecting duty on goods imported into Isle of Man. Net customs revenue is shared between the island and the UK on a proportional population basis. A notional figure is arrived at for the total fiscal population of the island; this includes an allowance for visitors based on decennial tests in which the actual imports of various commodities are ascertained, under the provisions of the Revenue Returns Acts of 1894–5. Thus in 1929 the actual visiting population was 599,048 and the fiscal equivalent was 38,156; this, added to the resident population of 49,078, gave a fiscal population of 87,234. The

68

Manx share of such customs duties as were imposed in both countries was calculated in the proportion of 87,234 to the total population of the United Kingdom. If, for any reason, Manx duty was different for any article, this would not be included in the Common Purse, but would be collected separately.

The Common Purse is still in force, despite minor changes in legislation and the adherence of both the United Kingdom and the Isle of Man to the European Economic Community. It was extended to cover purchase tax and, later, value added tax. A recent economic survey has, however, urged reconsideration of the Common Purse arrangement.

While financial problems have not been the only ones in the way of constitutional development, there is no doubt that the desire for financial independence has been very much at the root of the modern movement for increased Manx self-government.

THE CONSTITUTION

In 1911 the McDonnell Committee, appointed by the British Home Office, reported on the constitution of the Isle of Man and recommended certain changes. The first of these was that the tenure of the lieutenant governor be limited to a seven-year term. The other recommendation concerned the Legislative Council.

Legislative Council

This body had existed in some form from an early date—there are references in 1422 to the Lord's Council, though at this time it was evidently an executive council which collected the revenue and helped the governor to manage his affairs, keep records and so on. Gradually the council changed its function as the deemsters were added to it, followed by the Lord's Attorney (now the attorney general) and the bishop, archdeacon and vicar general, representing ecclesiastical interests. The

composition of the council varied from time to time, but its
function became that of a consultative council for the governor
and it gradually came to act as a second chamber of the legislature, all its members being appointed. In 1910 it consisted of
the bishop, Clerk of the Rolls, two deemsters, attorney general,
receiver general, archdeacon and vicar general. It began to
meet in public for the first time in 1882.

The McDonnell Committee recommended that the council
consist of ten members, exclusive of the lieutenant governor.
Four should be *ex officio* members, namely the bishop, two
deemsters and Attorney General; four should be elected by the
House of Keys either from their own members or from the body
of electors, and two should be appointed directly by the lieutenant governor, after the results of the Keys elections were
known. These changes were effected by the Isle of Man
Constitutional Amendment Act of 1919. By this time the office of
Clerk of the Rolls had been united with that of First Deemster.

The Legislative Council was presided over by the lieutenant
governor as the official head of government and representative
of the Crown. One change the McDonnell Committee did not
recommend was the setting up of an advisory council to help and
advise the lieutenant governor on legislation and procedure.
Earlier governors had probably used such committees in an
informal way. In 1927 the then lieutenant governor asked the
Keys to appoint a consultative committee, and his successor too
called on such a committee. During World War II the lieutenant governor had weekly meetings with his advisory committee,
primarily to deal with issues arising from the war, but later
including wider issues of insular government. This proved of
such value that at the end of the war the Home Office agreed
that the lieutenant governor should be assisted by an executive
council, composed of seven members of Tynwald, the majority
being the chairmen of the five principal spending departments
or boards, each of whom was elected.

The inner harbour, Douglas, at low tide (*author*)

Kipper processing. The true Manx kipper is cured in the smoke of oak chips (*Manx Press Pictures*)

Salting herrings as they are unloaded from a trawler in Douglas. Herring are emptied into a trough, where salt is thrown on them, and they are then shovelled into casks (*author*)

Isle of Man Act (1958)

The period since 1945 had seen the granting of independence to a large number of British colonies and dependencies. Not unnaturally the demand for further emancipation has grown in the Isle of Man and a series of commissions, reports and legislative acts has resulted. The Isle of Man Act (1958), passed in the Commons, repealed all the earlier acts concerning revenue, in particular the 1866 act. Henceforward control was much more firmly in the hands of the island legislature. Tynwald could impose, abolish or vary any customs duties; the lieutenant governor could do likewise by order, so as to make the Manx duties conform to those of the United Kingdom, provided Tynwald ratified the change within eighty days. An Accumulated Fund was set up with the aid of a £250,000 grant from Westminster and any surplus from the general revenue was paid into it. Payments out of general revenue could be authorised by act or resolution of Tynwald, with the lieutenant governor's concurrence; and the lieutenant governor was to present the island's budget to Tynwald in June each year. He therefore still held a key role in financial affairs.

Changes in the legislature

In 1958 the lieutenant governor set up a commission under Lord McDermott and, on its recommendations, considerable changes were brought about in the legislature. The appointed members of the Legislative Council were abolished, making way for two more elected representatives; the Second Deemster's seat on the council was abolished; and the powers of the council to block legislation were curbed.

Two new bodies were set up: the Finance Board—'to share and eventually to bear the governor's financial responsibility'— was to be *primus inter pares* among the various boards under Tynwald. There was also to be a statutory Executive Council consisting of the chairman of the Finance Board, four other chairmen of boards and two appointees of the lieutenant governor; this was

E

later changed to two elected members of the Legislative Council and five from the Keys, with the chairman of the Finance Board an obligatory member of the latter. The lieutenant governor still had the right of veto over Finance Board proposals.

Two other off-shoots of the McDermott Report were the creation of a Police Board, again leaving the governor with a veto on the direction and disposition of the Constabulary; and the formation of an Isle of Man civil service under the ultimate control of the governor.

The growth in the last two decades of multilateral international agreements has affected the clarity of the distinction between the responsibility of the United Kingdom government for the Isle of Man's external relations and defence on the one hand, and the island's domestic economy on the other. In 1966 —following the imposition on the Isle of Man, against the wishes of the Keys, of United Kingdom legislation, after a Council of Europe decision to restrict pirate broadcasting— a joint working party of Tynwald representatives and Home Office personnel, under the chairmanship of Lord Stonham, Minister of State, recommended certain courses of action; some of these, including the establishment of a 'Standing Committee on the Common Interests of the UK and IOM', have been implemented.

The latest report on the island's constitutional position is that submitted to the royal commission under Lord Kilbrandon in 1970. It seems unlikely that this will result in any radical change.

PRESENT-DAY GOVERNMENT

A distinctive organisation of government functions has taken shape in the Isle of Man—which is part of the British Islands but not of the United Kingdom. It can most accurately be described as a Crown dependency. The Crown, acting through the Privy Council, has the ultimate responsibility for good government. The Home Secretary is the member of the Privy

Council primarily concerned with Manx Affairs and he is the channel of communication between the Manx government, the United Kingdom government and ultimately the Queen. At the beginning of each reign, the Privy Council creates a committee with special responsibility for Manx affairs and this committee considers all Manx legislation submitted for the Royal Assent and any petition to her majesty from Tynwald. The Crown has ultimate control over the island on all matters pertaining to public order and the administration of justice; and the Westminster Parliament can, if need be, legislate for the island. In addition the lieutenant governor, as representative of the Crown, is head of the insular executive, with final control both of finance and the police. Parliament usually restricts its legislative powers to such matters as defence, shipping and aerial navigation.

The lieutenant governor has no power to give the royal assent, which can only come via the Privy Council; and his powers are more limited than hitherto. He has the power of veto on the Finance Board, but cannot force it to pursue any particular policy against its will. He is now helped and advised by the (relatively) new Statutory Executive Council, which functions as a sort of Cabinet. Following another recommendation of the McDermott Report, he no longer attends meetings of the Legislative Council as a matter of course, but still presides over Tynwald.

Legislation may be initiated either by the Legislative Council or by the House of Keys, meeting separately; but it can be finally approved only by a full meeting of Tynwald Court, after both branches have agreed to it.

Boards of Tynwald

The boards of Tynwald constitute a distinctive way of exercising central control of the public services and utilities. Most of the boards are entirely manned by members of Tynwald, but in some of them outside members are included, usually for

75

commercial or business reasons. Each board has its own executive permanent staff and officers, technical experts and usually its own premises. They issue annual reports which are printed and available for public comment. The boards fall into two categories: Government boards, such as those dealing with finance, harbours, education, local government, health and social services, agriculture and fisheries, highways and transport, tourist, civil defence, police and assessments; and semi-government boards—dealing with airports, electricity, water, forestry, mines and lands, and the Manx Electric Railway—which have outside participants.

THE LAW

The Manx high court, separate from that of the UK, is constituted with two deemsters, both appointees of the Crown. In appeal cases they are joined by a judge of appeal, who must be an English barrister and Queen's Counsel. The principal law officer is the attorney general, also appointed by the Crown. The Supreme Court of Appeal for the island is the judicial committee of the Privy Council. Many minor legal matters are dealt with, as in England, by sixty-two Justices of the Peace.

RELATIONSHIP WITH THE EUROPEAN ECONOMIC COMMUNITY

Following Britain's entry into the Common Market in 1973, the Isle of Man became an associate member of the Community, on the same basis as the Channel Islands. The island does not contribute to EEC funds, nor is it eligible for aid from those funds. Manxmen cannot avail themselves of the EEC provisions relating to free movement of persons within the Community.

On the other hand, EEC rules regarding customs and quantitative restrictions apply to the island, just as to the United Kingdom. Duties are to be progressively reduced for goods coming from EEC countries and for agricultural products and commodities processed from them. Levies and other import measures laid down in Community rules and applicable by the UK must also be applied by the Manx government to third countries. The EEC rules, as necessary to allow the free movement and observance of normal conditions of trade in these products, are also applicable to the Isle of Man. Subsidies creating unfair competition are not permitted.

5   THE MANXNESS OF MAN

BECAUSE the Manx people have been a relatively self-contained community living undisturbed by invasion for 800 years, their racial composition has been of fascinating interest to anthropologists. Anthropometric surveys have been made on several occasions: in the 1930s, for example, a sample of 1,200 men was studied, all four of whose parents were native Manx, and whose families were known to have been living in the Isle of Man before 1800. Curious and statistically significant differences were found in the various districts of the island. In the north—Jurby, Andreas, Bride, Ballaugh, Lezayre, Maughold and Lonan—and also in part of the south —Marown and Malew—there were significantly more fair than dark men. Rushen and Arbory in the south, Patrick in the centre and Michael and German in the north showed no particular differences, while the Douglas area had more dark than fair men. The predominance of fair men in the north is attributed to the fact that the Vikings settled in that region, on the best farming land.

POPULATION

In 1776 the population of Man was 14,027. For seventy-five years it increased steadily, to 52,000 in 1851, and then stabilized at between 52,000 and 55,000 at each census until 1931 when it sank to 49,000. The lowest point for over a century was reached in 1961 when it totalled only 48,113. Since then a brisk increase has been recorded to 50,000 in 1966; 54,581 in 1971 and over 60,000 in 1976.

Up to World War I the number of births regularly exceeded the number of deaths, but during the last fifty years there has been an excess of deaths, apart from the five years immediately after World War II, when, as elsewhere, there was a birth-rate boom in the island. In the period 1925–1970 the birth-rate crude average was 14·4 per 1,000 and the death rate 15·9. This suggests an ageing population, as the island's medical services are extremely efficient. The trend continues: in 1971 there were 2,454 births and 2,901 deaths—of which 2,726 were of people over sixty-five.

The age distribution of the people in 1961 and 1971 is of some interest:

Age group	1961	1971
0–9 years	6,024	7,667
10–19	6,364	7,004
20–29	4,315	6,845
30–39	5,374	5,419
40–49	6,203	6,320
50–59	7,605	7,325
60–69	6,633	8,520
70–79	4,137	5,295
80 and over	1,478	1,894

These figures show a considerable increase in the over-60 age groups; a stationary position in the 30–60 group, and an increase also in the under-30 population. Obviously immigration is involved here, otherwise the 0–9 group in 1961 would be roughly equivalent to the 10–19 group in 1971—and similarly for the older groups.

New residents

The census returns show that the number of people actually born on the Isle of Man has tended to diminish over the years. In 1881 there were 46,000; by 1961 only 32,345 out of a population of 48,113, and in 1971 32,374 out of 54,581. In recent years the Manx government has embarked upon a policy of attract-

79

ing new residents to combat the depopulation trend. In particular, income tax was kept at a low level: 21.25 per cent, with no surtax; and death duties were abolished. The island therefore became a tax haven for certain classes of people. Between 1958 and 1966, 6,363 new residents arrived; between 1966 and 1971, 8,258 more, and an estimated 10,000 between 1971 and 1976. So that since 1961 while the population has increased by some 12,000, over 24,000 new residents have settled on the island. Disquiet is now being expressed at this situation as clearly the number of immigrants must soon exceed the number of native-born islanders if present trends continue.

Newcomers have been settling in the island for over a century. It has always been a pleasant and quiet haven for retired people. Even more attractive was the seemingly lucrative tourist trade which, particularly before and after World War I, brought many people, mostly from Lancashire, to take over hotels and boarding houses.

Emigration

In the years before World War II and for a time afterwards there was a serious problem of winter unemployment in the island, although plenty of temporary, seasonal work was available during the tourist season. As there was nothing much in the way of industry to provide employment in the off-season months a programme of road improvement was begun which has paid dividends in the form of a first-class modern road system. From the early 1950s a policy of attracting industry to the island was embarked upon. Nevertheless the number of Manx people emigrating to the mainland remained— and remains still—quite high. This is partly due to the fact that young people must go away for their higher education; only recently has a college of further education been opened on the island, but anyone wishing to become a doctor, engineer, scientist or teacher must be trained on the mainland. The chances of such students, after qualifying, returning to the Isle of Man are problematical, though undoubtedly the lower rates of income tax are a considerable incentive to those who can find posts there.

Imbalance

The population therefore tends to be an ageing one. This was somewhat exacerbated by the policy of attracting new residents. An analysis of the Manx economy carried out in 1970–71 states that 85 per cent of new residents (heads of households) have incomes differing little from the average; and 46 per cent of new resident households were headed by retired persons with average incomes, who, after purchasing their houses, had relatively small accumulations of income which might be employed in generating capital investment. An ageing population gives rise to higher expenditure on hospital and geriatric services which has to be met by taxation of both the working and —so far as is possible—the non-working or retired population. The island government's programme of encouraging new industries was aimed originally at eliminating winter unemployment, but this has almost entirely disappeared in the last ten years or so. In fact, new industries face a problem of labour shortage and in the 1970s the government was stressing the need for capital-intensive rather than labour-intensive industries.

Housing

The major effect of in the influx of new residents has been in the sphere of housing and construction. The demand for property has been very strong for over a decade, and prices of private houses, particularly those of modern type, have more than kept pace with Britain. Young married couples had serious problems. There are no building societies in the Isle of Man and interest rates are controlled at a lower level than in Great Britain; however, the government stepped in with loans at a favourable rate for newly weds.

It is sometimes said that 'come-overs', as new immigrants are dubbed by the islanders, often become more Manx than the Manx—a phenomenon not unique to the Isle of Man. It is open to question, nevertheless, whether the justifiably esteemed 'Manxness of Man' would be maintained in the face of the continued entry of new residents—particularly if they were in the higher income groups and therefore more cosmopolitan in outlook. The 'Manxness of Man' has been under pressure from outside influences ever since the island was thrown open to the tourist boom of the nineteenth century. Nowhere is this more clearly shown than in respect of the Manx language. This is one of the variants of Gaelic which are found on the western fringes of Europe—from the Hebrides and Ireland to Wales, Cornwall and Brittany.

Written language

There is nothing extant in written Manx before Bishop Phillips's translation of the *Book of Common Prayer* which was compiled in 1610; it existed only in manuscript until the end of the nineteenth century. The remarkable absence of written material has been explained by the fact that the island was ruled by foreign aristocrats, first from Norway, later from England; the wealthiest people in medieval times were the heads of the various religious communities, who would be versed in English and Latin, but probably considered Manx not worth their attention. So the use of Manx in written documents and the development of a characteristic orthography (as in Ireland) never really arose.

It was Bishop Wilson, at the end of the seventeenth century, who began to write and publish in the vernacular. He produced *The Principles and Duties of Christianity* in Manx in 1707. (There is said to have been an earlier printed book, *The Ballad*

82

of Mannanan Beg Mac-y-Leirr, but this is only hearsay.) In 1722, when Bishop Wilson was imprisoned for two months with his vicars general, they improved the shining hour by translating the Bible into Manx. No part of this was published until 1748 when St Matthew's Gospel appeared; the rest of the translation came out in instalments up to 1773. The *Book of Common Prayer* was issued in 1765. The Methodist Hymnal dates from 1795 and the early followers of Wesley often used Manx in their meeting houses. Original writings in Manx still amounted to only a few religious works and some ballads.

The spoken word

In 1764, a pamphlet published by the SPCK stated that most of the 20,000 inhabitants of Man were ignorant of English. The first serious attempt to assess the number of Manx-speakers was not made till 1875, and showed that, out of a population of 41,000, 12,350 spoke Manx and 190 knew no English. Manx-speakers declined to 4,598 in 1901; 529 in 1931; 355 in 1951 and 165 in 1961. There has been nobody in the island for over 50 years who could speak no English.

In an introduction to the 1859 edition of Kelly's *Manx Grammar*—which was itself a pioneering effort—the Rev W. Gill stated:

> the decline of the spoken Manx within the memory of the present generation has been marked. The Language is no longer heard in our courts of law . . . in the Churches, the language was used by many of the present generation of clergy 3 Sundays in the month, then on alternate Sundays, and is now entirely discontinued in most of the Churches. In the schools throughout the Island Manx has ceased to be taught; and the introduction of the Government system of education has done much to displace the language. It is rarely heard in conversation except among the peasantry . . . It is a doomed language.

The current wave of concern about the Manxness of Man has caused a revival of interest in the language: for example, in

Peel, street names are given in Manx and English. There is little danger at the moment of the language dying out altogether because there are those anxious to maintain it. The fate of small minority languages is a problem not confined to the Isle of Man; it is, too, a question of conservation in a context not so universally accepted as are the usual aspects of this currently overworked word.

Origins of Manx names

Manx differs from Irish in being a good deal more phonetic, presumably because it was not written until modern times. Many words are almost identical with Irish, and there are also obvious affinities with Scottish Gaelic—in fact the language has been described as a dialect of Scottish. The prefix 'Mac', meaning 'son of', has been abbreviated in Manx to the simple C or K sound, thus giving rise to a preponderance of names beginning with C, K and Q, such as Cain, Collister, Corrin or Corran, Callow, Cannell, Clucas, Curphey, Kelly, Kewley, Keggin, Quayle, Quiggin and Quirk. These have all come from the Gaelic, but Norse names have similarly been incorporated into the language: Asmundr became Casement; Thorliotr became Corlett; Ottarr, Cottier; Thorketill, Corkill. Manx names are extremely characteristic and do not seem to arise elsewhere.

Place names too are both Celtic and Norse in origin. Ellan Vannin, the Manx name of the Isle of Man, is the Gaelic for Mannin Island. All places beginning with 'Balla' are derived from Gaelic: Balladoole, farm of the black stream; Ballameanagh, the middle farm; Ballamodha, farm of the dog. Douglas was so called from the rivers Dhoo (black) and Glass (grey or bright) which meet above the town and flow into the harbour. Castletown is the anglicised version of the Gaelic name. Peel is a Gaelic word for fort, though it was formerly known as Holmetown (Island-town), a Scandinavian name, and its Manx name today is Purt ny Hinshey (also Island Town). On the other hand Ramsey or Hranfsaa is from the Norse for 'Raven's Isle'. Norse

84

place names, ending in 'by', 'dale', 'fell' and 'wick', include Sulby, Jurby, Dalby, Druidale, Foxdale, Snaefell, Garwick and Fleshwick.

Although Manx is more phonetic—to an Englishman—than Irish, there are many variations from this. Consonants are generally similar to English but vowels vary quite a lot. Diphthongs also have different pronunciations. In addition there are the phenomena of mutation, aspiration and eclipsis, which also occur—and to a greater extent—in Irish. As in Irish, too, some constructions from Manx may still be found in the English conversation of Manx people. And a few Manx words and phrases are still treasured in everyday contexts, such as the *Thie Veg* for 'the smallest room in the house'!

Manx music

There has also been a resurgence of interest in Manx music in recent years. Much has depended on the oral tradition, as printed and manuscript sources are sparse. A collection entitled *Mona Melodies* was published in 1820, containing thirteen of the best-known songs and dance tunes. The poet, T. E. Brown, a famous Manxman, writing an introduction in 1896 to A. W. Moore's *Manx Ballads and Music*, observed that the class structure of Manx society prevented the emergence of a bardic class, or any royal or feudal tradition favouring such a development. Under the Stanleys the Manx were more like serfs than peasants, and the 'baleful effect' of the Church discipline of Bishops Barrow and Wilson, and the later influence of Methodism, had turned people away from music.

As against this, Chaloner, writing in 1650, noted that 'The Manx people are much addicted to the music of the violyne' so that 'there was scarce a family in the Island but more or less can play upon it; but as they are ill composers, so are they bad players'. This may have been occasioned by the strangeness of the music to English ears. Instruments were scarce; it is said that 'flutes made from the elder tree' were used in rejoicing when Bishop Wilson was released from prison in 1722. In 1812, writing of the harvest festival or Mheillea, Quayle states 'English country dances are unknown—jigs and reels with 4 or 5 couples joining take their place' and comments on the similarity of the airs to Irish ones.

Recent interest in traditional Manx music has borne fruit in a number of recordings, some in the Manx language. To the innocent ear, the songs have resemblances to both Scottish and Irish airs, with none of the special characteristics of either. Of special interest are the so-called *carvalyn Gailcagh*, which are old melodies set—relatively recently, in the nineteenth century— to religious words. Although termed 'carols', they do not have the traditional form associated with the English carol. The most popular Manx tunes are 'Ellan Vannin' (Isle of Man)—a nineteenth-century composition—and 'Ramsey Town', which is also not a folk melody of any antiquity.

The island today is rich in choral societies and has an annual choral festival.

Traditional customs

The most interesting island custom—'Hunt the Wren'—took place on St Stephen's Day (Boxing Day); this also survived until very recently in Ireland. A group of young people, carrying something to represent a wren—a casket with a bunch of feathers or even a branch of a tree with a few streamers on it— would sing a song describing the chase and eventual killing of the bird; this was related by characters known as Bobbin, Robin, Dickon and Jack-of-the-land.

The harvest festival, or Mheillea, is still celebrated, though not with the reapers carrying the image of Ceres as in days gone by.

Stories of the 'little people' are common in island folk tales and few Manxmen would drive over the Fairy Bridge at Ballalona, near Ballasalla, without wishing 'good morning' to the fairies.

In recent years the citizens of Peel—dressed in horned helmets and with approximations to the Viking longships—have re-enacted the first Viking landing in the island. This has hardly become part of the island's folk lore—as yet!

ISLAND SERVICES

The Isle of Man has its own radio station, Radio Manx, started by private enterprise but now under government auspices; it has also in recent years taken over control of its own coinage and postal services.

Posts and coins

The island's post offices were formerly sub-offices of the British GPO. Now that the service is under insular control, the authorities have made use of the postage stamp not only as a means of revenue, but also as a way of publicising the island. A considerable number of special stamps have been issued—even commemorating the centenary of the Douglas horse trams. Distinctive coins have also been minted—of exactly the same shape as their British counterparts, but featuring the Three Legs of Man, the Tower of Refuge and other Manx institutions. British and Irish coinage is freely accepted on the island, but letters sent from the Isle of Man must bear the postage due in Manx stamps.

Social services

The island's social services conform very much to the pattern in the UK, providing unemployment and sickness and maternity benefits; widows' and guardians' allowances; special allowances for the children of divorced people and widows; retirement pensions and death grants. From 1948 new legislation was introduced in line with that of the UK. An Industrial Injuries Act replaced the old Workmen's Compensation Act; and family allowances were introduced, as in Britain. There is general reciprocity with the United Kingdom regarding National Health Insurance and kindred matters.

The care of old people is becoming an ever larger concern of the social services. In 1954 4,775 people were receiving retirement pensions; by 1969 this had increased to 9,800. There is already an increasing demand for accommodation in homes for the old and infirm.

Health

There are twenty-three medical practitioners, thirteen district nurses and six health visitors on the island. The main hospital, Noble's, in Douglas is as fine and as modern a building as would be found anywhere. There are others, too: Ramsey Cottage Hospital and the White Hoe; also Ballinamona, at the Strang, catering for the mentally ill. Patients may, when necessary, be sent over to England for treatment, usually to a convenient place in the Wirral in Cheshire. The financial burden of health care has increased markedly in recent years—to some extent as a consequence of the age structure of the population.

ORGANISATIONS AND SOCIETIES

The number and variety of organisations in the Isle of Man is surprising, even bewildering. Twenty-four of these are concerned with welfare, ranging from the Family Planning Association to the Ramsey Home of Rest, and devoted to the care of the blind, the deaf, the disabled, children, sailors and old horses. There are national cultural organisations, such as the World Manx Association, the Isle of Man Natural History and Antiquarian Association, and Friends of the Manx Museum and Manx National Trust. The eighteen trade unions with sections in the island range from teachers to distributive workers and from seamen to health service employees. Rotary Clubs exist in Douglas and Ramsey, and also a Past-Rotarians Club.

Women's organisations include the Soroptimists; Inner

right: Pillar Cross, Maughold churchyard. Dating from the thirteenth-fourteenth centuries, this bears the first-known carving of the Three Legs of Man (*Manx Press Pictures*)

below: Cashtal yn Ard: near Maughold, a Neolithic burial ground. Formerly covered over and entered via the opening between the two stones in the centre (*Manx Museum*)

Castle Rushen showing the gate house, with the curtain wall, and the keep in the background (*Manx Press Pictures*)
St German's Cathedral within the walls of Peel castle. A thirteenth-century structure, which fell into disuse in the eighteenth century (*Manx Press Pictures*)

Wheels at Douglas and Ramsey; the Isle of Man Federation of Women's Institutes; Townswomen's Guilds; the Business and Professional Women's Club, and the National Council of Women. There are numerous forces organisations, mostly of ex-servicemen, and the Youth Training Corps.

There are seventeen agricultural associations; eight dramatic societies, and some sixty or more general organisations of a voluntary character, including seven musical societies, mostly connected with choral singing; Esperanto, philately, and photography are catered for and there are some political associations, such as the Fabian Society; the nationalist party, Mec Vannin; and the Ratepayers' Association. It has been said that nothing is easier in the Isle of Man than to attend some sort of society meeting every night of the week.

SPORT

Sporting organisations number no fewer than thirty-nine, ranging from an Everton Supporters' Club to the Samurai Jiu-jitsu and covering cricket, rifle shooting, angling, judo and karate, rock climbing, riding, swimming and sailing.

Apart from the association football supporters who commute regularly to watch Liverpool, Everton and even Manchester United, there are two divisions of the insular football league, representing all parts of the island. Rugby commands a smaller but equally enthusiastic following.

There are six golf courses—at Pulrose outside Douglas, at Ramsey, Peel and Derbyhaven, and at Port Erin and Port St Mary; thirteen Crown Bowling greens—this is a popular sport on the island; six swimming pools and eleven tennis court sites. Squash rackets has made its appearance and there are courts at Jurby and at King William's College. Hockey and athletics also have their devotees, but the islanders have never really taken to the traditional Gaelic games of hurling, or shinty, and Gaelic football.

There is a preponderance of motoring, motor-cycling and cycling clubs—not surprisingly in view of the leading part these sports play in the Isle of Man where all forms of reliability and speed trial take place.

TOURIST TROPHY RACES

The Royal Automobile Club began holding reliability trials for cars, over a 50-mile course, in 1904, to select competitors to represent Britain in the Gordon Bennett Cup. Similar trials were held in 1905, and in September of that year, the RAC started a Tourist Trophy race for cars, over four laps of just over 50 miles each. Forty-two started and eighteen finished the course, which ran almost round the island. A shorter course: Douglas–Peel–Sulby–Ramsey, was introduced in 1906. The motor race continued sporadically until 1914 and was revived in 1922.

By this time interest had switched to the motor cycle. The first motor-cycle race was held in 1907, on 28 May, when twenty-five competitors started and ten finished the course—then a very short one in the west of the island, based on St John's. In 1911, the mountain course was adopted and two races were introduced for motor cycles of different horse-power. With slight variations the course is the same today and covers $37\frac{3}{4}$ miles.

The TT course

The course starts on Glencrutchery Road, about a mile from Douglas Promenade and near St Ninian's Church. It proceeds via Bray Hill and Quarterbridge Road to the right-angle bend at the Quarterbridge, where it turns west over Braddan Bridge, through Union Mills and along a fairly straight road to Ballacraine. Here the road branches north and a tricky section begins, past Glen Helen, up Creg Willey's Hill and downhill at Barregarrow to Kirkmichael. A fairly straight run from here

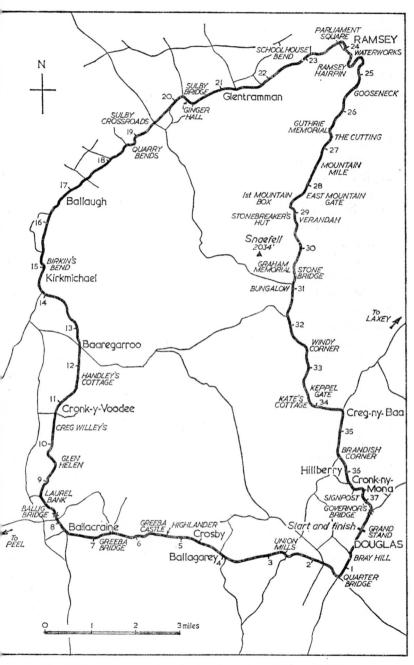

The full mountain circuit for the Isle of Man TT Race,
as it has been used since 1920

to Ramsey is interrupted by the bridge at Ballaugh and by the Quarry bends. The course runs through Ramsey town and up to the Ramsey Hairpin, followed by the Gooseneck, a right-hand bend on a steep slope. Soon the course emerges on to the mountain. The road passes through the Bungalow, halfway up Snaefell, through minor bends, to Windy Corner; the next descent is to the famous Creg-ny-Baa, a right-hand, right-angle bend. Brandish and Hillberry Corners are next, neither of them as difficult as of old; finally comes Governor's Bridge, an acute hairpin bend, but only ¾ mile from the finish of the course, and the start of another lap.

When the races began, the island roads were by no means tailored for road racing. The intervening years have seen tremendous improvement in surfacing, the ironing out of many bends and the flattening of hump backed bridges; in fact, everything has been done, within reason, to eliminate undue hazards while retaining the sporting character of the many corners, hills and bridges. The first race was won at an average speed of 38 mph. By 1939 the more powerful machines (500cc) were averaging about 85mph and since then the 100 mph 'barrier' has been passed. Nowadays the races are varied: the traditional 500cc, 350cc and 250cc classes, with a race for side cars; a race for machines of 125cc has also been held.

At one time, practice took place between 4–6am during the week or two before the races. At present, the roads are closed later in the day, usually in the early evening. This is justified because so often mist and fog occur in the early hours.

Champion riders

The TT races have their own hagiology. The names of Stanley Woods, Alec Bennet, Wal Handley and Fred Dixon between the wars, and of Geoff Duke, John Surtees, Phil Read and the Italian Agostini in the post-war period are held in great reverence by those who enthusiastically follow the machine-age sport of motor-cycle racing.

Currently the races have been eliminated from those which count towards the world championship, but it is hard to imagine that this will dim their popularity.

The TT race was always patronised by the manufacturers of the machines, so that the riders were all professionals. In 1923 a race began for amateurs, riding more or less ordinary production machines. The Amateur TT lasted for only a few years and was replaced by the Manx Grand Prix. The Official TT takes place early in June; the Manx Grand Prix in September.

COMMUNICATIONS

SHIPPING

THE sea has always been the principal feature of the Manx scene—as a way of life for its inhabitants and as a career for those who chose to see the world. Men of Manx descent were on the *Bounty* with Captain Bligh—the name, Christian, of the chief mutineer, is a typical Manx surname. Manxmen fought in the navies of the American Civil War and men and ships from the island were at Dunkirk, Algiers and Normandy in World War II.

As a means of communication with neighbouring parts of the UK and Ireland, the sea has been of major importance. The age of steam brought about an acceleration in the development of links with the mainland. Before that, the voyage under sail was usually attempted from the nearest point, which in Britain is Whitehaven, in Cumberland. The prevailing westerly winds often made the passage very difficult whereas, if the wind was in the east, landing on the eastern shores of the island—where most of the harbours lay—could be awkward or indeed impossible.

With the advent of the steamship, the Isle of Man became a stopping place for steamers sailing between the Mersey and the Clyde. The formation of the Isle of Man Steam Packet Company in 1830—the first crossing being made on 14 August—placed things on a regular basis and ensured the reliable, safe and even comfortable travel which has endured to the present day.

The Steam Packet Company

The Manx people's own shipping line is now approaching its

150th anniversary. Other shipping companies—often operating on a much wider scale—have been forced out of business or into channels other than maritime ones. Yet still the red-funnelled Manx boats ply their trade year in and year out. In an age of air travel the era of passenger ships would seem to be nearing its end, but there is no sign of this in the Isle of Man, although one-third of passenger transport has passed into the hands of the airlines.

The Steam Packet Company's fleet of relatively small ships, around 2,500 tons, ploughs on through summer and winter, calm and storm, war and peace, carrying many millions of people each decade, with a loss of life that by any standards is unbelievably small and an almost negligible accident rate—an unexampled record of consistency, reliability and safety. Not surprisingly the Steam Packet Company and its steamers have become a legend. The development of the company has been eagerly followed in the island—and indeed far beyond. The advent of a new vessel is almost a national event and the ships themselves have become the object of intense interest and affection.

The Isle of Man Steam Packet Company was inaugurated at a meeting on 17 December 1829 in Dixon and Steele's Sale Rooms in Douglas, on Douglas Harbour, when a committee was appointed 'with instructions to ascertain the probable cost of a steam packet'. The sum of £4,500 was subscribed on the spot. The committee went to work with a will and ordered a new vessel, *Mona's Isle*, from John Wood of Glasgow, with engines by Robert Napier. She cost £7,052, and bore a tall funnel, red with a black top, which has been the company's distinguishing feature ever since, antedating the adoption of the same colours by the Cunard line. The early vessels were wooden paddle steamers, the *Mona's Isle* being 116ft long by 19ft in the beam. Increasing traffic necessitated regular additions to the fleet in 1832, 1834, 1842, and 1845, then every few years thereafter. The names of the vessels have for the most part been perpetuated

97

in their successors: *Mona's Isle, Mona, King Orry, Ben my Chree* (Girl of my Heart), *Tynwald, Mona's Queen, Snaefell.*

The first iron ship was the 1845 *Ben my Chree*, and the last the *Fenella* of 1881, which was also the second screw steamer. The last paddler was the beloved *Empress Queen*, launched fittingly in 1897 and wrecked on the Isle of Wight in World War I. The turbine era began in 1905 with the *Viking*, which ran for the company until 1954, with interludes of service in two wars. The increase of traffic in the years before 1914, and then the loss of ships in the war caused the company to buy a number of ships ready-built rather than to the company's design, these included some ex-railway company steamers.

Further losses in World War II and a rather ageing fleet of steamers brought a policy of regular and rapid building, and ten passenger ships were built between 1945 and 1976. The last four of these were passenger-carrying car ferries, the latest two being diesel engined. Today there are seven passenger ships; of these the car ferries run throughout the year so that winter travellers are carried in the newest—and fastest—of the fleet and not, as in days gone by, the oldest and slowest. Out of the company's seven ships, all but two are semi-permanently laid up from September till late May. Formerly the fleet used to winter at Barrow but nowadays it lies up in the Great Float on the Cheshire side of the Mersey.

The seasonal nature of the traffic to the Isle of Man has always created special problems. For over eight months of the year, only two passenger vessels are needed to perform the daily runs between Douglas and Liverpool. There was a time before World War I when the island had links with a considerable number of British and Irish ports. At some time of the year, there were direct passenger sailings to Llandudno, Liverpool, Fleetwood, Heysham, Blackpool, Whitehaven, Barrow in Furness, Silloth, Garliestown, Ardrossan, Glasgow, Belfast and Dublin. On the island, Douglas, Ramsey and Castletown have all been used for passenger traffic, while Peel and Port St Mary handled cargo. That choice has been whittled away and today passengers may travel by steamer only from Liverpool and Fleetwood in England, Ardrossan in Scotland, Llandudno in Wales, and Belfast and Dublin in Ireland. Only from Liverpool is a regular daily service maintained all the year round, or even at the height of summer—at which time Fleetwood and Heysham previously had a daily link. This may be attributed to increased air traffic and the growing economic difficulties of sea transport.

Some of the Isle of Man steamers have run for fifty years, others for about twenty-five; thirty-five is a reasonable average. For a ship engaged in summer service only, it would then have completed the equivalent of about ten years' continuous running. About 2,000 passengers can be carried but full capacity is generally reached only at weekends. Formerly the company ran three cargo steamers, but now two container vessels maintain a nightly service between Liverpool and Douglas five nights a week. Light cargo in vans and lorries is also carried by car ferry.

This is the Isle of Man Steam Packet Company's sailing schedule for a mid-season Saturday—24 July 1976:

Lady of Mann	Douglas to Liverpool	(Friday)	2355
	Liverpool to Douglas		0900
	Douglas to Ardrossan		1500
Mona's Queen	Liverpool to Douglas		0100 (1st)
	Douglas to Liverpool		am
	Liverpool to Douglas		1100 (1st)
	Douglas to Liverpool		1600
Ben my Chree	Ardrossan to Douglas	(Friday)	2330
	Douglas to Liverpool		0830
	Liverpool to Douglas		1530
Manx Maid	Liverpool to Douglas		0100 (2nd)
	Douglas to Liverpool		0730
	Liverpool to Douglas		1230
Manxman	Liverpool to Douglas		1000
	Douglas to Belfast		1630 (1st)

	Belfast to Fleetwood	pm
Mona's Isle	Douglas to Liverpool	am
	Liverpool to Douglas	1100 (2nd)
	Douglas to Belfast	1630 (2nd)
	Belfast to Stranraer	pm
Snaefell	Douglas to Liverpool	0900

Although this would not be the busiest day of the season, twenty-one different and separate sailings are undertaken by the seven vessels, one having to steam only the 80 miles from Douglas to Liverpool, while the *Mona's Queen* makes the crossing no fewer than four times during the day. Three journeys are without passengers so as to have the vessels in the right places for succeeding operations. In the whole week 23–30 July, there were no fewer than 100 ship movements. The maintenance of services on this scale, on a stretch of water not noted for its docility, is an achievement that is easy to underestimate. But only once, in the winter of 1909, has a Steam Packet ship been lost with fatal casualties—when the *Ellan Vannin* foundered in the Mersey approaches on a violently stormy night.

Other shipping lines

Direct competition with the Steam Packet Company has usually been short, if sometimes vigorous. For many years, Railway Company steamers sailed from Heysham and Barrow to the island, but never on the Steam Packet's 'own' routes. For almost eighty years a steamer sailed from Dublin to Silloth via Douglas, mainly carrying cargo.

Today there are two other shipping lines in regular operation: a container service sails out of Castletown harbour, and the Ramsey Steamship Company, founded in 1913, is still in business with a handful of ships, with names such as *Ben Varrey, Ben Veg* and *Ben Seyr*. The company was responsible for the maintenance of food and water supplies to Radio Caroline when that station was moored a few miles off the Manx coast at Ramsey in the early 1960s.

COMMUNICATIONS

Interest in commercial air traffic to the Isle of Man dates from the early 1930s, the first flights being from Blackpool and Liverpool. Numerous companies were involved and by 1938 over 10,000 passengers a year arrived and departed by air. The island's airport was established on the south-eastern plain at Ronaldsway, adjoining Derbyhaven. After military use during the war, it was finally handed over to the Manx government in 1948, and placed under the direction of the Airports Board of the Manx legislature. The airport has expanded over the years, as the pre-war DH Rapide gave way to the post-war DC3 and later to the Viscount and BAC 111, and as traffic increased— new terminal buildings being erected in 1953.

Nowadays, the main traffic routes are operated by British Airways to Liverpool, Manchester, London and Belfast. Other lines fly from Blackpool, Dublin, Glasgow, Leeds, Newcastle and Edinburgh; and there are summer services from Bristol, Cardiff, Prestwick, Carlisle, Birmingham and Teesside.

This shows the comparable number of arrivals by air and by sea in 1975:

1975	*Air*	*Sea*
January	8,202	2,731
February	7,385	2,492
March	10,891	8,645
April	11,429	6,335
May	23,393	47,251
June	29,799	65,438
July	31,420	113,096
August	34,789	114,540
September	23,088	47,099
October	13,300	8,096
November	7,512	3,906
December	7,961	5,345

The pattern of air traffic is distinctly less seasonal than that of sea arrivals, and in winter more people come by air than by sea. Nevertheless there has been some decline in summer air traffic in 1974 and 1975 from the level of 171,559 reached in 1973.

ROADS

For the last seventy years, special attention has been paid to the improvement of roads, which is partly attributable to the island's long connection with motor-cycle and car racing. The work was undertaken as part of a scheme for providing winter employment for a population largely based on a seasonal tourist industry, so that over decades Manx roads have progressed to a remarkable extent—not only the main trunk roads between towns and on the motor-cycle TT course, but also the network of minor roads. Those in the heart of the northern uplands, from the TT course near Windy Corner to Barregarrow near Kirkmichael, and the branches off it to Druidale and Ballaugh on one side and to Injebreck and Douglas on the other, provide examples of this improvement. Stretches of country are now open to the motorist which formerly were frequented only by the hiker or cyclist.

The care and development of the roads is in the hands of the Highways Board. In 1972 it watched over a total of 420 miles of classified roads. Traditionally the necessary finance has been raised in a curious manner—by diverting to the Road Fund the revenue from all sorts of licences: auctioneers, brewers, pedlars, dogs, driving tests, gun and game; also public service vehicle and all motor and driving licences, and until 1958 even liquor licences. The income in 1973 from such sources was £242,000, while the cost of road improvement and maintenance alone was £420,000, and there were other expenses. The number of licensed vehicles in 1973 was 26,114; three-quarters of these were private cars—about one to every three inhabitants.

Road Traffic Commissioners, introduced in 1966, issue

licences for public service vehicles and also regulate parking places and even stopping places for buses.

The longest journey in the island can be undertaken in less than an hour, so there is no need for modern motorways. The road system is very adequate with some very beautiful drives round the coast and in the central uplands.

TRANSPORT

Motor buses came to Douglas as early as 1914, but operated strictly within the then rather restricted bounds of the borough. In 1926, they were introduced on the promenades and about the same time replaced the cable cars to Upper Douglas in the winter. The following year a Cumberland firm started an island-wide bus service; this began an era of intense competition, which ended when the island's own company, Isle of Man Road Services, absorbed two competitors in 1929. Today buses are the only form of public transport, apart from the very restricted service of the Manx Electric Railway. Douglas corporation services, which spread out as the town grew, have been integrated with Isle of Man Road Services, in the interests of economy. In 1976, the Isle of Man National Transport Company was founded to operate all public transport.

Isle of Man Railway

Archaic forms of transport have always been one of the island's attractions. The oldest of these is the Isle of Man Railway. The company, registered in 1870, proposed lines connecting Douglas with Port Erin, Port St Mary and Castletown; with Peel, and with Ramsey. Talk of a possible steamer service from Port Erin to Holyhead at this time may have encouraged this rail project. Money was slow to come in, however, and the Ramsey line was abandoned. The line to Peel was opened in 1873 and to Port Erin in 1874. A separate company, the Manx Northern Railway Company, registered in 1878, constructed the line from St John's, near Peel, via Kirkmichael to Ramsey. There was a connection with the Isle of Man Railway at St John's so that it became possible to send through carriages from Douglas to Ramsey. A branch from St John's south to Foxdale was opened in 1886, largely based on the mine workings there; and the line failed when the mines ran out. The ore was carried from Foxdale direct to the quay at Ramsey. After a recommendation from Tynwald, the Isle of Man Railway bought out the Northern Railway Company in 1905.

The railway system really did very well for a long time, even after bus competition began in 1927. In 1901 there were about 700,000 rail passengers; in 1920 1,609,000; in 1937 this had fallen to 775,000, but even in 1950 1,076,000 were carried. The early 1960s brought increasing difficulties—partly economic, partly of a technical and maintenance character. The end came rather swiftly, after various partial and temporary closures, and the railway system closed down at the end of the 1965 season.

The enthusiastic Marquess of Ailsa revived the railway and ran it from 1967 to 1972. From this date the Railway Company again assumed control, with a government subsidy, but operating only between Douglas and Port Erin, By 1976 the once-flourishing, island-wide system was reduced to a summer service between Ballasalla and Port Erin. The rest of the permanent way—with girder bridges, rails and abandoned rolling stock—was sold as scrap.

The railway played an important part in the development of the island; it greatly improved the accessibility of the resorts outside Douglas—indeed it was from the time of its construction that such places as Port Erin and Peel, and even Ramsey which also had a direct steamer service, began to challenge Douglas as holiday centres.

The Manx Electric Railway

The tramways boom, at the end of the nineteenth century, based on the use of electric power, reached the island in 1893.

A single track was laid from Douglas, starting at the north end of the promenade and following a coastal route over the shoulder of Banks' Howe to Groudle, the first creek to the north of Douglas Bay. While still under construction it was acquired by the Douglas–Laxey Coast Electric Tramway with the aim of extending it to Laxey. This was achieved the following year and by 1899, the necessary powers having been obtained, the line ran as far as Ramsey.

Associated with this development but necessarily separate because it ran on a 3ft 6in gauge and not the 3ft gauge of the main line—was the Snaefell Mountain Railway, starting at Laxey and climbing to the summit of Snaefell, 2,000ft higher. This opened in 1895. Financial difficulties ensued after the collapse of Dumbell's Bank in 1900, and the Isle of Man Tramways and Electric Power Company, which had been running the Ramsey and Snaefell lines, failed.

The lines were then taken over by the Manx Electric Railway Company, together with the associated glens and hotels. Tynwald had insisted on an all-the-year-round service when the Ramsey extension was agreed to, and until 1975 it was in operation, Sundays excepted in the winter months. The company ran into difficulties in the early 1950s and there were threats of liquidation until the government took over in 1957.

The Snaefell branch has only operated in the summer season since its inception. At the end of the 1975 season, the line from Laxey to Ramsey was discontinued—a great pity, as the Douglas-to-Ramsey drive on the Manx Electric was surely the most exciting of the few tramway routes remaining in the British Isles, even counting the Snaefell ascent. The line interweaves with the main road from Douglas to Ramsey sometimes forging through wooded country, then bursting out on to the brow of startling cliffs; and views are attainable from the tramway that cannot easily otherwise be seen. Essentially it connects a series of glens along the rim of the island's rocky north-east coastline. Groudle, Garwick, Laxey, Dhoon, Glenmona, Ballaglass—all these are passed before the line turns inland from the headland of Maughold Head and drops down into Ramsey. The company's early success was due to the fact that, before the advent of motor transport, these beauty spots could only be reached by the Manx Electric Railway.

Horse trams

Possibly the most famous of all the island's variegated forms of transport is the horse tramway system in Douglas. This runs the whole length of the promenade, from what used to be Derby Castle to the southern end at Victoria Pier. The trams were started by a gentleman named Lightfoot in 1876, when the northern section from Summerhill to Broadway was opened. Extension to Peveril Square, adjoining Victoria Pier, was approved in 1877. The tramway was acquired in 1894 by the Isle of Man Tramways and Electric Power Company which also owned the electric lines to Snaefell and Ramsey, and there was some idea of an integrated system from Victoria Pier to Ramsey. After the collapse of this company, the Douglas corporation bought the line along the promenades.

For many years the horse trams have worked only in summer. The 1¾ mile journey takes twenty minutes; no horse does more than four return trips daily. The rolling stock has varied a good deal over the years—from open 'toast racks' to semi-closed two-decker tramcars, but today they are all single decked. From time to time proposals have been made to replace the tram system by an augmented bus service, but good—touristic—sense has prevailed.

HARBOURS

In 1771 an act was passed in the British Parliament 'for repairing, amending and supporting the several harbours and seaports of the Isle of Man'. This was an early recognition of the importance of the Manx harbours, not only for the inhabi-

The 'New Iron Pier' at Douglas, from an engraving. During its thirty
years of existence, it was a centre of recreation and amusement. It
closed in 1903

The annual sitting of Tynwald at Tynwald Hill, which takes place
on 5 July. The various ranks of the legislative hierarchy are on
succeeding levels of the terraces (*Isle of Man Tourist Board*)

Laxey Wheel, the Lady Isabella, greatest relic of the island's mining history, was commissioned in 1854, and recently rehabilitated after half a century of idleness (*Manx Press Pictures*)

tants but, at that time, for shipping in general. Omitting Port Erin, which is no longer a commercial harbour, then only Peel of the Manx ports is on the west coast. Douglas, Castletown, Ramsey, Port St Mary and Laxey all lie on a rather exposed east coast.

Douglas Harbour
A Family Tour through the British Empire, published in 1804, describes how the family—presumably fictional—set out from Dumfries to sail to Dublin and were forced by storm to shelter in Douglas. In the early nineteenth century a notable resident in the island—though not a Manxman—was Sir William Hillary, who lived at Fort Anne, overlooking Douglas Harbour. He is best known for being the founder of what became the Royal National Lifeboat Institution; and he was assiduous, even fanatical, in his attention to matters pertaining to safety at sea. One of his pet schemes was the construction of a large 'Central Harbour of Refuge' at Douglas, serving the whole of the Irish Sea. The development of the steamship and its rapid increase in size and safety rendered this idea obsolete. However, Douglas Harbour has continued to command attention and controversy even to the present day.

About two-thirds of all Manx cargo traffic and virtually all seaborne passenger traffic goes through Douglas, so that the development of its harbour facilities has been of major interest. Its east coast situation has always caused problems when the wind is easterly, though the harbour is well protected from the prevailing winds which, on average, are from the west-south-west. As early as 1826, Hillary proposed a long breakwater in a northerly or north-north-easterly direction. Besides the hazards represented by strong inshore winds, the harbour was beset with rocks. On one of these, Conister Rock, in 1832 Hillary took the initiative in building a castellated structure; the Tower of Refuge is one of the landmarks of the Isle of Man to this day. The other mass of rocks, the so-called Pollack Rocks,

G 109

became less significant when the Victoria Pier was built, partially upon them, in 1872.

The original pier at Douglas was roughly at the site of the present Steam Packet Company cargo wharf at the entrance to the inner harbour. It was built in 1793 but was replaced in 1832 by the Red Pier, a pleasant structure with a circular end surmounted by a lighthouse. Until the Victoria Pier was built forty years later there was no landing of passengers direct to the quay unless the tide was relatively high. It the absence of an effective breakwater, both the Red Pier and Victoria Pier were mercilessly exposed to easterly winds. A 600ft breakwater had been built out from Douglas Head in 1864, but this inadequate wooden structure was partially demolished by storms in January 1865 and finally disappeared in 1867. The building of Victoria Pier was the first use of Portland cement in Douglas Harbour. The present breakwater, or Battery Pier, was begun in 1879 and finished in 1883. It has lasted to the present day though not without problems. Easterly gales over the years have caused erosion and reinforcement has been necessary. In the late 1880s Victoria Pier was lengthened by 400ft to its present length, allowing two steamers to berth on each side. In 1930 work began on the Red Pier extension scheme which provided two more non-tidal berths; this, the King Edward VIII Pier, is one of the few monuments so named in that monarch's short reign. A swing bridge guards the entrance to the inner harbour. This section is completely tidal and ships are high and dry at low tide. At the inner end of the harbour, the river Douglas enters on the south side, and there is a stone pier, known as the Tongue, which used to be the winter berth for one or two of the Steam Packet vessels. The water area of the outer harbour is 30 acres; it is said to be able to accommodate vessels up to 10,000 tons at all states of the tide, though it is doubtful if this has ever been done. There are 3,000ft of low-water berthings available for passenger vessels. In addition, the Battery Pier can also accommodate cargo vessels and trawlers. The harbour entrance—the space between the Battery and Victoria Piers—measures 470ft and faces north-east. The tidal position here is curious as the set is in a southerly direction both on the ebb and the flood. The flood stream is north-east, from Langness to Banks' Howe, but there it splits and the westerly half circulates round Douglas Bay across the harbour entrance and then rejoins the main stream. The ebb stream does not bifurcate in the same manner and is consistently southerly.

Douglas Harbour is still inconveniently open to easterly winds. Fortunately, in summer, when traffic is heavy, strong winds are more commonly from the west. In face of an easterly gale, ships sail into Peel harbour. With the opening of a passenger terminal building in 1965, would-be travellers no longer have to wait for hours in inadequate shelters on the pier, as used to be the case.

A survey of Manx harbours in 1972 recommended the building of an open-piled structure between King Edward VIII Pier and Victoria Pier, to provide extra berthing and a storage area. It also put forward a proposal—one which had been repeatedly shelved in the past—to extend the breakwater, recommending that it incorporate a cellular structure which might be used for oil storage. The 1972 cost of this proposed extension—which has increased considerably since it was first mentioned in 1925—would have been £3½ million.

Other harbours

After Douglas, Ramsey harbour is possibly the most imposing, with 3,000ft of quay and a water area of 20 acres. At the entrance there is a 70oft masonry pier on the south side, and on the north side a timber breakwater, also 700ft long, built in 1855. Like all Manx harbours, it is tidal and ships are high and dry when the tide is low.

Peel Harbour, of similar size to Ramsey, is at the mouth of the river Neb, which here flows north. There is a strong breakwater at the outer end of the harbour, running south-west to north-east; so this is the best-protected harbour in the island. Its main value is as an alternative to Douglas for the ferry service from the mainland; for the import of oil for the generating station at Peel; and for the fishing industry, though this may have declined somewhat owing to the development of fishing grounds off the island's east coast.

Castletown, Port St Mary and Laxey are all small harbours, the first two much patronised by pleasure craft. In terms of trade, Castletown stands next to Douglas. In 1955, the Isle of Man's imports totalled 200,000 tons and exports 24,000 tons. Douglas handled 70 per cent of both; Ramsey 12 per cent of imports and 25 per cent of exports; Castletown 3½ per cent of imports and no exports; Peel about 5 per cent of both. By 1975, 319,607 tons were imported and 57,615 exported. Douglas handled 72 per cent of both; Ramsey's share had fallen to 3–4 per cent, but a new container service brought Castletown 15 per cent of imports and 20 per cent of exports.

LIGHTHOUSES

There were lights on the Calf of Man, in Douglas Harbour, Castletown and Derbyhaven in the eighteenth century. Modern developments start with the act of 1815 which enabled the Commissioners of Northern Lighthouses to erect lighthouses on the Isle of Man and the Calf. Within three years there were lights on the Calf of Man and at the Point of Ayre, designed by Robert Stevenson. The light on the Calf was replaced in 1875 by one on the Chicken Rock. This was seriously damaged by fire in 1960 and subsequently fog and light signals were made automatic. In 1968 another light on the Calf itself, facing west, was put into operation.

The lighthouse on the Point of Ayre is still operating; it stands at the northern tip of the Ayres, the northernmost point of the island. The lighthouse at Langness, adjoining Derbyhaven, dates from 1880.

Douglas had a light on the end of the old pier which was of

dubious value to judge by early accounts. In 1832 the first lighthouse was built on Douglas Head and was rebuilt in its present form in 1892. The latest addition to the island's lighthouses is the one at Maughold Head, dating from 1914.

Lighthouse	Height over sea level	Signal
Point of Ayre	106ft	Alternate red and white flash every minute
Calf of Man	306ft	Flash every 15 seconds
Chicken Rock	125ft	Flash every 5 seconds
Langness	76ft	Double flash every 30 seconds
Douglas Head	104ft	6 flashes every 30 seconds
Maughold Head	212ft	Triple flash every 30 seconds

In addition there are numerous signal lights of a minor type round the coast at: Point of Ayre; Peel Harbour (4); Port Erin (3); Port St Mary (2); Castletown (2); Derbyhaven; Douglas piers and harbour (5); Laxey, and Ramsey (2), with four flashing signals on the various sandbanks north-east of Ramsey.

7   THE VISITING INDUSTRY

TOURISM—or the 'visiting industry' as it is often called in the Isle of Man—while basically an offshoot of the industrial revolution in Britain, is of very long standing.

EARLY VISITORS

Originally people visited the island mainly for its sea bathing and the therapeutic effects of its undoubtedly bracing climate. Colonel Richard Townley, a Lancashire gentleman who sailed from Whitehaven to Douglas in 1789, made some amusing comments on holidaymaking at that time. Even then 'great numbers of strangers are visiting this island, either for pleasure, curiosity, or the hopes of recovering lost health'. He mentions the arrival of a gentleman 'with a most sickly debilitated appearance . . . I fear he will soon be bound for a more distant country . . . from whose bourn no traveller returns'. But a month later he was climbing Douglas Head with the same gentleman who was able to 'ascend that height without difficulty and walk there a considerable time'.

Townley stayed a year on the island, occupying his time by walking round Douglas and riding to more distant places. He describes visits to St George's Church, to hunt balls and card parties, and also took great interest in the fishing industry. He records how many times the mail boat was held up by bad weather or managed to beat out into Douglas Bay a few vain miles before having to return. He does not say very much about his bed and board beyond conceding that 'strangers may live at all times as well in the eating way as reasonable people can desire'.

There was a lively theatrical life; a band of players arrived from Ireland and opened with *The Imposters* by Mrs Inchbald. The amateur theatre also played its part, though Townley is rather scathing about the results. Another evening he went to a 'childish entertainment—*Ombres Chinoises*', a musical affair with silhouettes of the singing characters. In June 1789 a firework display was spoiled by adverse weather.

The general impression from Townley's account is of a few score of visitors in a fairly small village, interesting themselves as best they could in local industries, antiquities, and the innocent public amusements of the time. Even as he wrote, the steam engine was beginning to spread the first effects of the industrial revolution and, from 1810 onwards, steam paddle-boats appeared in the coastwise traffic.

First guide books

The first visitor's guide book to the Isle of Man, compiled by Robert Haining, appeared in 1822 'designed as a companion to those who visit and make a tour of it'. The author estimates that 'during the last two summers we have had a great influx of visitors, computed at about 3,000. Many come for pleasure and a few to recruit their shattered constitutions. They circulate considerable sums of money.' By this time three steamboats were calling at the island en route between Liverpool and Greenock or Dumfries, and two more were being built at Liverpool. 'Considerable preparation has been made for the accommodation of visitors by enlarging the inns and increasing the number of lodging houses': the principal inns were listed and 'furnished apartments in private houses may be procured from 7/6 to one guinea per week'. By 1832, in a later edition of his work, Haining lists nine hotels and thirty-two lodging and boarding houses.

There were considerable difficulties in travelling to and from the island despite the greatly enhanced reliability of the steamboats. Douglas Harbour could be entered only at certain states of the tide and it was normal for passengers to be landed by small boat. The pier built between 1793 and 1801 was regarded from the outset as grossly inadequate as a protection against the sea and was used mainly as a fashionable parade for the local people.

According to Jefferson's *Guide* of 1823, every person leaving the island had to procure a pass or permission from the governor 'which may be got at the Steam Packet Office, John Clarke, Douglas, for ninepence'. Without this, the traveller might lose his passage or the captain of the vessel carrying him be liable to a fine of £10. Travelling was not a cheap pastime—the fare from Liverpool to Douglas was £1 in the cabin or 10 shillings steerage.

The sea crossing

Various steamers and sailing packets had been providing a reasonable enough service during the summer months, but during the winter only one company had continued to serve the island—the St George Company, which ran slow and small boats 'shameful hulks, devoid of shelter and accommodation other than that of a small cavern aft, and what screen there might be on the lee side of a singularly tall funnel'.

The Isle of Man's population had doubled from 20,000 to 40,000 in sixty years, and it was the need for communication by sea on a regular basis which led to the formation in 1829 of the Isle of Man Steam Packet Company. Its new steamer *Mona's Isle* carried fifteen saloon and seventeen steerage passengers on her first voyage on 14 August 1830, and took eight hours for the crossing from Liverpool to Douglas. Passengers still had to be embarked and landed by small boats. As there was competition from various shipping companies, boatmen and porters were hired to direct passengers into particular packets. This led to scenes of some disorder at Liverpool with 'shouting, bawling, pulling, tearing, cursing and swearing'. The voyage once begun, passengers were entertained by 'batches of drummers and fiddlers', often the sailors themselves; or the traveller might divert himself with cheese and porter, and by playing backgammon, or 'gazing vacantly around o'er the dark blue sea, lost in thought and feeling in the recollection of the past or anticipation of the future'. Meals seem to have been included in the fare and there was a precipitate rush for the cabin when the dinner bell was rung.

Competition led to price cutting. The Manx people were loyal to their own company and had passed a resolution that if the Steam Packet Company pledged itself never to charge fares over half a guinea, the public would bear the loss even to the extent of collecting in churches. The Steam Packet Company began by charging a single fare of only 5 shillings (saloon) and 3 shillings (steerage); the St George Company, increasingly competing for passengers, was eventually reduced to issuing a sixpenny one-way ticket.

Island amenities

What diversions awaited the passengers arriving by the new steamers? Bathing was still paramount; one account refers to the sands 'on which about this time commence the ablutions of thousands from a twelve months accumulation. . . . Droves of raw Lancashire men and women are seen simultaneously dipping together, like devotees along the banks of the Ganges'. Evidently the ladies wore bathing dresses but the men were not invariably covered, and the contemporary writer advocated separation of the sexes—and even the wearing of bathing costumes distinctively coloured according to sex.

Travel within the island was not very organised. A twice-weekly, round-the-island coach trip was tried in 1823 but failed. Tourists preferred to travel in gigs or on horseback. By the mid-1830s more regular coach services were running . . . the *Governor* to Peel; and the *Express*, *Eclipse* and *North Star* to Ramsey.

There is a report of a regatta in Douglas Bay in June 1830

at which '30 pleasure yachts from all parts of the channel' were present. By 1836 housing development had begun in Douglas, where the population was then 8,000. The range of 'beautiful marine villas and terraces called the Crescent' ending at Derby Castle at the north end of the bay had just been completed, and the beach wall opposite to it. The southern end, however, round Sand Street (later Strand Street) and Fort Street was 'a line of mouldering hovels'. There was 'no public recreation, except we speak of a concert now and then made up for the benefit of some lazarette or cabbage water establishment'. The stage, too, had been in decline for some years. A letter of 1846 states that there is not a theatre in the island, and performances were largely amateur efforts.

Sir George Head reported in 1840 how the traveller on arrival in Douglas faced 'a number of obtrusive agents for the inns . . . who after the manner of touters belonging to stage coaches, stand like a swarm of horseflies in his way, each holding the respective card of his establishment under his nose'. The porters, though now subject to control, had formerly rendered it 'impracticable without an effort of strength, or coming to personal issue with the offender, to prevent luggage and parcels being forcibly carried away, one knew not by whom or whither'. Head warmly praises the British Hotel where 'my table was crowded with viands actually in despite of my own remonstrance in a degree of profusion quite incompatible with the reasonable charges on the bill'. Some hotels began to set up billiard rooms and, by 1858, Kerruish's *Guide* notes that 'a quarter mile from Castletown is Collins' American Bowling Saloon'. In the same year, John Morley, evidently from Bradford, built the Theatre Royal in Wellington Street, Douglas, seating 1,000.

GROWTH OF TOURISM

Significantly, about this time the number of guide books to the island proliferated considerably—indirect but strong evidence of the growth of tourism. The Steam Packet Company now had four steamers in service; the return fare was 9 shillings first-class and 4 shillings and sixpence second-class.

By 1874 there were six steamers, with fares amounting to 10s 6d and 5s 6d. A sailing from Ramsey to Whitehaven had started and another company was operating a daily service from Barrow in Furness. There were occasional sailings from Silloth in Scotland and from Dublin operated by the North British Steam Packet Company. Coach travel within the island had also improved; there were two coaches a day in each direction between Douglas and Ramsey, and Douglas and Castletown, with connections to Peel, Port Erin and Port St Mary. From 1873 onwards the railway took over as the main means of transport. In the same year, the opening of the Victoria Pier permitted for the first time the direct landing and embarkation of passengers at all states of the tide.

The number of visitors had risen from 20,000 to 30,000 annually in the 1830s to about 60,000 in the 1860s. In 1873—with the new landing facilities—there were 90,000 visitors; this number doubled by 1884 and in Jubilee Year, 1887, almost doubled again to 348,000. Although this was an exceptional year, steady growth followed, reaching its peak in 1913 when well over 600,000 visitors landed on the island.

By 1878, positive efforts were being made to enable the visitor to pass his time pleasantly. In Douglas, where construction of the promenade had been begun in 1864, 1,000ft of roadway, 75ft wide, had been completed, despite difficulties and destruction by heavy seas. This was fairly adjacent to the ladies' and gentlemen's bathing grounds, the charge for a machine being 6d. For those who did not wish to immerse themselves in the sea, there were the Marine Baths, in Marina Road, and the Mona Hydropathic Seawater Baths in Castle Street. Port Skillion Gentlemen's Bathing Place, at the foot of Douglas Head, had just been completed.

The Iron Pier—built in 1869 near the promenade, opposite

where the Villa Marina stands today—had seats and a refreshment room; charges were 1d a visit, 1s 6d a month or 5s per annum. In the evenings dances were held at the end of the Victoria Pier, and at the Douglas Head Hotel, there was a dancing platform open 3–10 pm during the season, admission 3d, with a quadrille band in attendance.

Opposite the Iron Pier and leading up to the top of the town was the wide thoroughfare of Broadway, with the British and American Bowling Saloon on the corner. Not far up the hill, just off Broadway, was Handley's Bowling Green Hotel and open-air skating rink. There were bowling greens also on Douglas Head and at the Quarter Bridge; and Handley's Hotel also boasted a croquet ground and billiard saloon. Altogether there were seven billiard saloons and four American bowling saloons. A race course at the Strang, a mile beyond Kirk Braddan Church, had been opened in 1870, a race meeting being held in August each year. The races subsequently ceased to pay and were discontinued; the course was occasionally used thereafter by the bicycle club.

None of the other towns in the island seem to have made efforts comparable to those of Douglas to cater for the amusement of visitors. Peel, Castletown and Port Erin were still small fishing villages, even though Castletown was the traditional seat of government. Ramsey, in the north, aspired to emulate Douglas; it was 'a favourite with many of the best educated classes who frequent the Isle of Man'. Reasonably well supplied with hotels and lodging houses, Ramsey had direct sea communication with both Liverpool and Whitehaven. Its south pier was lengthened by 550ft to provide shelter for the embarkation and landing of passengers travelling by steamer.

TOURIST ACCOMMODATION

The period from 1880 to 1914 was one of feverish growth in the Manx tourist trade. Whereas in the 1830s there was less than one visitor annually per head of population, by 1913 there were no fewer than twelve. Even had these been spaced evenly over the year, they would have constituted a strain on accommodation; largely concentrated between June and September they posed an ever-growing problem to those engaged in the hotel and boarding-house trade. In the 1830s, about sixty lodging houses and hotels advertised in visitors' guide books; by 1852 there were eighty, and the *Manx Sun* reported in 1870 that there were 1,500 lodging houses in Douglas alone. An act for the well ordering of lodging houses, which passed through Tynwald in 1865, provided for the inspection and licensing of such premises and for subsequent registration. The keeper of such a house had to provide a 'certificate of character for honesty and sobriety' signed by three householders. A proper supply of water was insisted upon; also adequate cleansing of all parts of the house, and precautions to be taken in the event of infectious disease occurring.

In 1895 the *Isle of Man Times* published a list of accommodation for visitors, which shows that towns outside Douglas had now become conscious of their tourist potentialities. Whereas there were 93 establishments listed for Douglas—apparently not including any on the sea front—Ramsey had 104, Peel 53, Port Erin 52 and Port St Mary 43. The official Board of Advertising soon took over publication of the accommodation list. After World War I, the figures were: Douglas 400 establishments, Ramsey 65, Peel 91, Port Erin 68 and Port St Mary 36, with 61 in Onchan. Not all the island's boarding houses figured on the list, however.

A comparison of charges shows a slow rise in the cost of accommodation up to 1939. In 1895 hotels on the promenade were charging 6s 6d to 8s 6d a day, all in; whereas a boarding house in Victoria Street was available for 5s or bed only for 1s 6d. There was plenty of accommodation available at £1 to £1 10s per week. In 1913 some hotels on the promenade were charging 5–7s a day, larger establishments perhaps 8s 6d to

10s 6d. On the other hand it was possible to stay in Walpole Avenue, near the pier, for as little as 4s 6d; and on Mount Havelock the charge was 4s for gentlemen, 3s 6d for ladies, with special terms for married couples. Young men could live well at the holiday camps—Cunninghams, above the Central Promenade, or Howstrake, on the side of Banks' Howe—for a little over £1 a week.

This was indeed the high summer of Manx tourism. In 1920 the Douglas Boarding and Lodging Houses Association fixed minimum charges of 10s 6d on the promenade and 9s 6d in other districts. Beds alone cost 4–6s on the promenade, and 3s 6d–5s elsewhere; with a charge of 2s per person for 'cooking and cruet'—as many visitors did their own food purchasing and had it cooked in the house. The Depression of 1930–3 forced prices down somewhat; in 1939 promenade hotels were charging 7s 6d–10s 6d a day and more modest boarding houses about 6s.

TOURIST ATTRACTIONS

In 1875 the Loch Parade—essentially a sea wall running north from Victoria Pier—was opened. The rest of Douglas Promenade was completed in the next two decades, and the terraces of houses, all without exception serving as private hotels, were erected. Ramsey and Port Erin followed the example of Douglas in this respect.

Organised amusements became increasingly important in the period before World War I. At the northern end of Douglas Promenade, Derby Castle, once the residence of the Pollock family, opened in 1877 as a ballroom and was extended and rebuilt seven years later—in 1971 it was replaced by a new entertainment complex. Derby Castle ballroom held 5,000 dancers; there was also a theatre where concert parties and variety held sway during the summer. Falcon Cliff opened in 1882—the hotel with its white tower still stands on the cliff top, halfway along the sweep of Douglas Bay; but the ballroom has long vanished. The Palace, just below Falcon Cliff, was opened in 1889 and is still in existence despite a destructive fire in 1920. The ballroom, said at one time to be the world's largest, occupies 16,000sq ft. There was also a theatre, similar to the one at Derby Castle, known as the Coliseum but this was demolished in the 1960s to make way for the gambling casino. In 1913 Douglas corporation acquired the Villa Marina, also on the promenade at the foot of Broadway. This had been both a private residence and a school at various times, but was now developed as a ballroom—'a magnificent Kursaal has been erected and equipped at a cost of £89,000'. In its first season, visitors were entertained by Herr Simon Wurms and the famous Imperial Viennese Band.

The Manx International Exhibition of 1899 was held at Belle Vue, outside Douglas, and this continued as an amusement park. The Isle of Man Racecourse was on the same location; it closed in 1929.

In the first *Official Guide* of 1896, Laxey Glen Gardens offered croquet and lawn tennis to tempt the ladies; a bowling green, bowling saloon and billiards for their male companions; also boating, cycling, swings and hobby horses, an excellent band and a restaurant . . . 'The Place to spend a Happy Day'. Groudle Glen—'the Fern Land of Mona'—advertised the Sea Lion rocks and the smallest passenger railway in the world. Golf links at Howstrake and Castletown are mentioned. Port Soderick modestly styled itself the most popular pleasure resort in the island; 'Romantic, Natural and the only FREE Glen on the Island . . . Smugglers Caves FREE'—and also music, dancing, boating and games.

The many glens of the island lay open to visitors with the construction of the railway from Douglas to Peel, Port Erin and Ramsey; and with the coastal electric trams to the north and the Snaefell railway. Sulby and Dhoon Glens made their appearance in the advertisements—the former already described as 'the Manx Switzerland'.

THE ISLE OF MAN

Apart from the sea bathing, bracing climate and undoubtedly beautiful scenery, one of the main attractions was the opportunity for sightseeing afforded by the island's rail and tramway systems. Other amenities were springing up as more and more people from the North of England began to take holidays in the summer and as there was a growing awareness that tourism had to be wooed if it was to develop.

Theatres appeared with a more permanent look than hitherto, such as the Grand, in Victoria Street, later to become a cinema. The Marina Ballroom became the Gaiety Theatre in 1900 and is now the only real theatre left. The Pier Pavilion, opened in Walpole Avenue in 1905, was turned into a cinema in 1927. A Camera Obscura came into operation on Douglas Head. Swimming pools were built in Port Erin in 1890 and Douglas in 1906-8.

The first TT motor-cycle race was held on 28 May 1907. From time to time, motor races have also been held, but the motor-cycle TT boasts the longest continuity of any such race; in latter years bicycles too have raced on the same course. These events take place in the earlier or later parts of the summer season so as to extend the peak period of tourist traffic.

World War I saw the end of the expansion phase; by then the shape of tourism in the Isle of Man had assumed its modern form. The natural beauties and amenities were to be increasingly supplemented by man-made artefacts. The motor car had not made much impact on internal traffic by 1914, but in the 1920s charabancs began to oust the old horse-drawn landaus and carriages from Douglas Promenade.

TRENDS OF THE TOURIST TRADE

In the period 1920-39 the number of visitors to the island varied considerably owing to economic and social conditions prevailing in the United Kingdom. Thus 1920 was a good year with 561,000 visitors; 1926—the year of the General Strike—a bad one with 385,000. Figures for 1930-2 reflected, though only

House of Keys, Prospect Hill, Douglas; the main Government offices are on the same site (*author*)

Inscription in Manx on a public bench in Peel (*author*)

Bilingual street name in Peel (*author*)

marginally, the effects of the Depression and averaged about 500,000. There was a distinct improvement towards the end of the 1930s. In the years following World War II, the peak figures for 1913 were at last equalled or surpassed. Since then there has been a general decline, though with considerable fluctuations. Air transport to the island, which started in the 1930s, did not contribute significantly to passenger returns till after 1946.

Bearing in mind the rise in population of the United Kingdom and, even more, the vast increase in the proportion of people taking holidays away from home, the Isle of Man has not by any means maintained its former share of the holiday trade. Not surprisingly, when the boom years of the late 1940s were followed by the slump in traffic of the early 1950s, the island began to take an intense interest in the basis and validity of its tourist trade.

1955 commission's report

In 1955 a Visiting Industry Commission recommended in its report: encouragement of early and late season visitors; rehabilitation of natural amenities, such as glens; standard of service and facilities to be raised, and first-class entertainment to be provided for a longer period. Other recommendations were that all hotels and boarding houses be graded and registered, and government help be given for modernisation. Changes in the rather restrictive licensing laws and shop-opening hours and regulations were suggested, such as limited Sunday opening of public houses.

An interesting statistical survey showed that 34 per cent of visitors to the island were under thirty years of age, compared with 27 per cent for United Kingdom resorts as a whole; and 61 per cent were persons of 'moderate income' compared with, for example, 48 per cent in Jersey. The average stay of a visitor was 10·7 days compared with 13 days in Jersey, which meant that there were relatively few who stayed for two weeks. Average expenditure was £18 per head against £32 in Jersey.

H

The most revolutionary feature of the report, however, was a recommendation that a gambling casino be set up in the Isle of Man. The fact that the island was Manx also needed to be emphasised: the Manx language ought to be used in street names; and greater use made of the island traditions and monuments, such as Tynwald and Castle Rushen.

Publicity Board

Government assistance to the tourist industry was administered by the Publicity Board, one of the executive boards of Tynwald. Expenditure by the board trebled in the decade 1951–61 from £33,000 to £96,000. Repeated pleas for more accommodation for the transport of motor cars to the island resulted in the Steam Packet Company introducing its first car ferry in 1962. Others were added in 1965 and 1972 (and 1976) so that a year-round car-ferry service became available. Car arrivals, which were 4,472 in 1961, increased to 6,539 with the first car-ferry sailings the following year. By 1966 the figure was 10,170, in spite of the seamen's strike of that year. In 1967, the first full year with the second ferry, the number was 15,948, and in 1973, the first full year with the third ferry it was 21,686; by 1975 it had risen to 23,600.

The powers of the Publicity Board had been considerably widened in 1958, partly to enable it to deal with the recommendations of the 1955 commission. From this time, a broader approach is noticeable and the government has stepped in when necessary to avoid the erosion of the island's tourist potential; for example, the famous Laxey Wheel was taken into public ownership in 1965, and the Gaiety Theatre, in imminent danger of closure, was purchased in 1971.

The 1970 report

It is significant that, while the 1955 commission dealt with the Visiting Industry, the commission of 1970 was reporting on Tourist Industry Development. The change in nomenclature

128

indicates a total conversion to the view that the Isle of Man was in an international and highly competitive industry. The 1970 report gives some important facts and figures. Estimated income from tourism was £14 million—half the national income. A great many of the 1955 recommendations had been implemented by this time. The casino had been built and, despite some unfavourable publicity due to events in its early days, is still in operation. The glens and other natural resources have been very well cared for and restored where necessary; a wildlife park has been established in the Ballaugh Curraghs; and a new passenger terminal built in Douglas.

The 1970 report called attention to the need for new accommodation for visitors: six new hotels were needed, with a minimum of 60 double rooms with bath; 500 new self-catering chalet units on five sites of 100 each, and 125 units of the motel type, in five sites of 25 each. Caravan parks have been strictly forbidden on the Isle of Man; the report urged reconsideration of this, while granting that chalets were preferable. Ninety per cent of the island's accommodation was in establishments with fewer than twenty-six bedrooms and there was need for modernisation. Development in various parts of the promenades in Douglas should be considered—a sign of the times was that in 1939, Douglas and Onchan together had six theatres, six cinemas and four ballrooms; in 1970 there was one theatre, four cinemas, two entertainment centres and the casino. At the same time, the provision of television shelters in Douglas was brought up for consideration, and the improvement of shopping facilities was urged as a matter of some priority. The need for education and training in catering was mentioned as an important factor, and the exploitation of the Manxness of Man again advocated.

The 1971 survey

Another report on tourism is included in the general economic survey made by a firm of consultants for the Manx government and published in 1971. This gave the information that 51 per cent of visitors were from North-west England; 12 per cent from North Yorkshire and Humberside; 8 per cent from the Midlands; 7 per cent from Scotland; 12 per cent from Ireland, north and south; and 10 per cent from elsewhere. The survey expressed the opinion that the island was associated to a possibly undesirable extent with tourists from the North of England, and that the image of Douglas loomed too large to the exclusion of the rest of the island—attracting some, but repelling others.

In an analysis of accommodation, the conclusion was that premises with over twenty bedrooms accounted for the lion's share—85 per cent—of tourist sales income. Including all its ancillary activities, such as transport and entertainment, tourism was still the main industry; as much was spent by visitors on beverages, entertainment, retail goods and travel as on accommodation. Action was urged to reduce the cost of travel, particularly in the 'shoulder months' of May and September. Owing to the growing influx of cars by the new ferries, provision of motel and chalet accommodation was again urged. Despite previous efforts to attract more annual conferences, this 1971 report did not altogether favour them. It did support maximum encouragement for the improvement of existing tourist accommodation.

The severe international competition in the tourist industry has been emphasised many times by commissions and surveys. Possibly the general drift of world economy may have a deciding voice. The rising price of oil has greatly increased the cost of travelling to the island as to many other places. Events may cause an abatement in the boom in Continental holidays, which would be to the benefit of the Isle of Man.

8   THE INSULAR ECONOMY

TOURISM, agriculture and fishery are the traditional economic activities of the island, to which nowadays may be added manufacturing industry, construction and commerce. Another major employer is government service—as is usually the case with small populations enjoying the institutions associated with independent government. Tynwald has shown a high degree of concern for the economic prosperity of the island and as well as the various commissions on tourism, there has been no lack of activity on the industrial manufacturing front, nor any reluctance to use outside help in this context. The Industrial Advisory Council, which reports twice yearly to Tynwald, is composed of two nominees of the governor, two elected by Tynwald, one nominated by the Isle of Man Chamber of Commerce, one by the Isle of Man Trades Council representing the Trade Unions, and finally one nominee of the Confederation of British Industry.

In 1970–1 a firm of international management consultants was invited to make an economic appraisal of the island with a view to shaping its development during the next generation. This investigation showed that the Gross National Product in 1969–70 was £32 million, with an average per capita income close to that of the United Kingdom. Primary sources of income were tourism, manufacturing, construction and net income from abroad. Net incomes in both tourism and agriculture were below United Kingdom levels, and agriculture made a very small net contribution to the national income. Capital investment was largely concentrated on dwelling houses rather than

131

the productive sectors, such as tourism. Wages and salaries tended to be lower than in the United Kingdom; employment was rising in the construction and service industries. Imports (including invisibles) exceeded exports (also including invisibles).

The survey showed that the economic support activities of the government in the basic sections of the economy were very substantial compared to the United Kingdom, Northern Ireland, the Irish Republic and Jersey. Agriculture has benefited very considerably from such activities.

AGRICULTURE

The lowland areas and plateaux round the coast, and the midland valley, support a mixed type of farming with some local variation. Mixed crop and livestock farming occurs in the north and in the coastal region between Ballaugh and Kirkmichael. These areas comprise sandy or sandy loam soils; they are also the driest parts of the island, with about 35in annual rainfall, and being well drained, tend to produce an early harvest. Here the average size of farms is above the normal for the island.

Dairy farming is the principal type in the island. Specialised dairy farming is practised in districts closely adjacent to Douglas, Ramsey and Port Erin. A large area of the south-eastern lowlands, north and north-east of Castletown, a smaller area near Peel, and the Maughold peninsula are all devoted to mixed farming with main emphasis on the dairy side. The specialised area round Douglas makes an important contribution to the demand for whole milk, especially for manufacturing. Cattle are predominantly Friesian and Dairy Shorthorns. Potato growing is an important subsidiary to dairying.

Mixed farming with emphasis on beef production is mainly centred on the western side of the northern drift lowland between Andreas and the sea, but also goes on in coastal regions near

Kirkmichael, on the Castletown plain and between Douglas and Ramsey. On the lower slopes of the southern uplands north of Castletown, and on the Patrick plateau south of Peel, mixed livestock farming is practised. Hill sheep farming extends widely on the northern uplands and to a lesser extent on the southern, though quantitatively it occupies a minor role. Manx lamb is greatly esteemed by both islanders and visitors and the stimulus of the ready market during the tourist season has encouraged early lambing—in the 1950s over half the farms began lambing before the end of January.

Reckoned by the number working in agriculture, the importance of the industry in the island has diminished sharply in the last 100 years. According to the census returns, in 1881 6,417 persons were engaged in agriculture and fishing. A steady reduction followed to 4,520 in 1901—of whom 3,656 were evidently working on the land. A temporary increase to 4,236 in 1911 was followed by a steady decline to 1,833 in 1961. An economic survey in 1971 gave a total of 1,250 employed in agriculture and fishery; and the same source estimates the contribution of this sector of the economy to the national income as 2·1 per cent.

The impression given is of a seemingly declining industry, but this is not a true picture. Farming in the island has a rather chequered history. The scale of operation has always been small. 150 years ago, most of the cultivated land was farmed by yeomen farmers with 10–150 acres of their own and only a small: minority exceeded 200 acres. There was a tithe system in force; transport, both internal and external, was poor and uncertain, and even in those days the island was a net importer of farm produce. The Tithe Commutation Act of 1840 liberated the industry from this annual burden. In 1860 the common lands were reorganised. Whereas previously landowners enjoyed rights of common on the moorlands of the upland regions and the Ayres—which included grazing, quarrying, and peat cutting—these had been encroached upon by the intack enclosures during the nineteenth century. The Disafforesting Act of 1866 provided that, after the deduction of 3,445 acres of intack existing within the old Forest Wall, the remaining 25,700 acres should be be divided, one-third to the Crown with no public rights; one-third to the people, vested in the Trustees of the commons, and one-third for sale, to provide money for development work, such as fencing—the latter was mostly purchased by the Crown.

The growth of the tourist trade and consequent expanding economy encouraged a more commercial attitude to farming. A five-course rotation was generally adopted—two years grass, one year oats, one year potatoes or turnips, and one year barley or oats, undersown with grass.

In 1866 there were 56,000 sheep and 9,000 cattle. The number of sheep rose to about 100,000 by World War II when it fell to 60,000; after the war it began to climb again. Cattle also showed an upward trend, apart from the period 1920–45. During the inter-war years, farming languished, arable land reverted to rough pasture and hill farms were often abandoned. By 1939 substantial amounts of milk and cream were being imported during the tourist season, though oats were being exported. During World War II, another 12,000 acres were brought under cultivation; after the war, there was an increase in the importance of ley pastures, and in 1957 there were 90,000 sheep and 18,000 cattle, and 44 per cent of the land was classed as arable.

The economic survey of 1971 found that there were altogether 965 agricultural holdings, of which about 16 per cent were under 10 acres, and another 41 per cent too small to provide full-time employment for one man. The number of viable farm units was given as 410. In fact, the survey showed that 24 per cent of the 'farmers' were no longer farming; 12 per cent did it only 'as a hobby', and another 12 per cent had sales of under £2,000. The number of agricultural workers was static at 470. By 1971

—a year or so after the survey was taken—the number of holdings had fallen to 935, of which 73 were over 300 acres. Figures for 1969 show that 1,300 acres were devoted to potatoes; twice as much to turnips; four times as much to both barley and oats, with minor acreages for wheat and vegetables. Sheep numbered 113,000; cattle 26,000 (with 7,000 cows in milk), and poultry included 25,000 broilers and 68,000 layers. By 1974 the number of cattle had increased sharply to 43,000, though the other figures were relatively little changed.

Besides emphasising that the industry was carried on in too many small units, the 1971 survey made the point that half the Manx farmers were over fifty-five years of age. Farm incomes were low at an average of £520 per capita—this was the average for agriculture and fishery—and one-third of this was due to government grants and support schemes. This compares with a figure at that time of £1,250 in the United Kingdom. Production was 'unrealistically orientated towards the home market' which could not absorb all the fatstock, milk and cereals. On the other hand, exports were not usually profitable, though a change in emphasis, towards specialising in cheese, seed potatoes and honey, was suggested. In general the industry was not sufficiently market-orientated. The guarantee scheme was seen as an obstacle to efficiency.

A new farm amalgamation scheme was recommended with built-in tests for improved productivity. Long-term government disengagement from the agricultural price and market system was another recommendation. The suggestion was also made that the Manx farming industry was overcapitalised because of its small size. Fields of over 20 acres are uncommon, especially away from the lowland areas; 10–12 acres is more usual, with many fields well below 5 acres.

The insular Board of Agriculture maintains an experimental farm near Peel, at Knockaloe, the site of the World War I prisoner-of-war compound.

FISHERY

The Manx fishing industry is best known to the rest of the world through the medium of the celebrated Manx kipper. The herring fishery has been the mainstay of the island fishermen for centuries, though many other fish are caught in surrounding waters—indeed, today shellfish have become more important for the indigenous fishing boats.

At the end of the eighteenth century, at least 340 Manx boats were fishing, mostly 12 tonners with a crew of seven or eight. There were two types of craft—the 'nicky' and the 'nobby'—in common use. Outside vessels came to the island to purchase herring from the native fishermen. By 1864, of the fishing boats at work, 290 were Manx, 300 Cornish and Scottish, and 100 Irish. The Manx boats also followed the herring round the Irish and Celtic Seas—to Howth, Co Dublin in October; Kinsale, Co Cork in March, and back to the Isle of Man in June. By 1914 the fleet was reduced to 57 luggers, of which 30 had auxiliary engines; crews numbered 350. After World War I the industry was in a decline, only 25 boats being left in service —19 at Peel and 6 at Port St Mary. Earnings per man had altered very little in more than a century and averaged only £20–£30. The number of Manx boats fell steadily from the 1920s onwards. Outside boats—particularly Scottish—increased in numbers; at first they were steam drifters and later motor drifters. In the 1930s ring netting was introduced and became the most popular method of fishing.

The fishing grounds were mainly south and west of the island; they extended for 20 miles, from 10 miles north of Peel down to the Calf of Man and within 10 miles of the coast, being mainly concentrated in the southern half, between Niarbyl and the Chicken's Rock—though an eastern ground between Douglas and Laxey was fished on a modest scale. Yields of fish varied quite markedly—from 21,159 crans in 1927 to 2,240 crans (a cran is 3½cwt) in 1934, averaging 11,000 crans annually from

1923–50. Medium-sized herrings gave ten 'long hundreds' (a long hundred is 124) to the cran; larger ones about seven. Many herrings were caught but removed to ports outside the Isle of Man, such as Port Patrick, Ardglass and Fleetwood. A report on the industry in 1950 notes the difficulty in recruiting crews; there were few experienced men available, and a shortage of suitable boats, so training of younger men was hard to organise. There was need for instruction in net making and repairing; in navigation and marine biology, and in the care of the internal combustion engine.

The island's kipper-curing industry was meanwhile in something of a decline. In the decade 1948–58 the number of curers fell from 14 to 6; and the number employed from 180 to 95. The number of packets of kippers sent from the Isle of Man—mostly by tourists while on holiday—showed a similar drop—from 366,000 to 203,000 over the same period.

A 1959 report on the industry recommended various measures to improve its prospects: from a direct subsidy to the improvement of the facilities and amenities for fishermen in Peel, improved marketing arrangements; quick freezing and cold storage; an apprenticeship scheme, and the re-establishment of a separate fisheries board—instead of integration with agriculture.

East coast fishing grounds

From 1964 a change came over the shape of the Manx fishery. Fishing on the east coast grounds in September and October became suddenly more important. The west coast fishery had been based on fish which actually seem to spawn off the east coast in the autumn. New methods of mid-water trawling allowed fishermen to take advantage of the migration of the herring to the east coast and a new industry has grown up based on this fishery and the use of Douglas Harbour as the centre of operations. During September and October, depot ships arrive to take on the large catches of herring, which are salted immediately.

This extension of the industry and the rising price of fish has meant that the total Manx herring catch has reached a figure around £1 million. It has also meant a much higher level of catch—almost 90,000 crans in 1970 and in 1974, when metric measure was introduced, 25,387 tonnes or about 140,000 crans. Such activities obviously carry their own dangers, and the certainty that the ground would soon be fished out brought restrictions on the duration of the fishing season. In 1973 fishing in the eastern grounds was banned from 1 October to 17 November to allow spawning to proceed. Even so, catches were still too high and an extended close season from 14 September to 17 November was recommended. Instead, a limit of 18,000 tonnes was agreed upon. Manx fishermen take very little part, however, in the highly organised and mechanised industry of today—in 1973 there were only five Manx boats in the herring fleet.

Shellfish trade

The islanders have been harvesting a different sort of produce from the sea: shellfish, in particular two varieties of escallop—tanrogans, *Pecten maximus*, and queenies, *Chlamys opercularis*. In 1968 catches worth £250,000 were taken by thirty-five boats. Queenies were introduced to the American market in 1969. By 1970 fishing for queenies was the most important branch of the island's fishing operation, for Manxmen. Again the spectre of overfishing looms large and it has been urged that more effort be turned to the herring fishery to ease the pressure on shellfish resources.

Marine Biological Station

Watching over and advising on the many problems of the fisheries in the Isle of Man is the Marine Biological Station at Port Erin. Established in 1892 by the Liverpool Marine Biological Committee, it has been under the aegis of Liverpool University since 1919. To quote from the British Association:

'The Port Erin Station is a seaside laboratory which enables the investigator to examine the sea bottom lying around the Isle of Man and to make known the conditions of existence and the various kinds of plants and animals living in the Irish Sea.' The station, situated at the foot of the cliff on the south end of Port Erin Bay, has been a teaching centre and also a fish hatchery, subsidised by the Manx government. It has played a major role in advising on technical matters concerned with the herring fishery. The annual report on the fishery emanates from the Marine Biological Station.

INDUSTRY AND COMMERCE

Manufacturing

Manufacturing incomes were estimated in the 1971 economic survey as being almost as important as tourism. The manufacturing industrial sector was dominated by one particularly successful engineering concern making specialised products. Labour shortage affected the possibility of industrial expansion and this was exacerbated by the effect of the high cost of housing on the recruitment of labour. Subsidised housing was recommended for new residents in essential manufacturing occupations. The cost of providing one new manufacturing job, at the time of the survey was reckoned at £6,000, including the provision of a publicly owned small house. Property values and building costs have since then increased considerably.

In 1970 there were ninety concerns employing 2,500 people in manufacturing; the specialised engineering firm was responsible for one-fifth of the total employed; 67 out of 92 firms employed fewer than 20 people and in only two cases were more then 250 employed. Engineering gave 40 per cent of employment; textiles 20 per cent; food, agricultural and fish products about 14 per cent; Printing 7 per cent; Quarrying and Building materials 5 per cent. The number in engineering was rising, but the opposite was the case in food products. This 1971 re-

139

port pointed out that the island no longer needed industry to provide employment, but rather to correct a progressive imbalance in the population structure. In 1974, 2,932 people were employed in 124 industrial firms, three-quarters of which employed less than 20 workers.

Construction

The construction industry enjoyed a considerable boom in the late 1960s and early 1970s, mainly in house building for new residents, but also in the erection of new public buildings. There were, in 1970, five large building firms, employing 600 people in all; eleven medium-sized ones, employing 500, and fifty-six small ones employing 250 workers. In addition there were electrical contractors, tilers, joiners, bricklayers, painters, plasterers and plumbers—occupying about 750 in all. The industry continued to expand and by 1974 over 2,800 were employed on construction.

New companies

An interesting feature of the employments of the population lies in the greatly increased numbers engaged in insurance, banking, finance and professional services. This can be related to the attempt to establish the Isle of Man as a tax haven. There has been an extraordinary increase in the number of companies registered in the island. In 1966–7, 170 new companies registered in a year. By 1969 this had doubled to 344; the following years saw an increase to 582, and then to the region of 1,000 for the next two years. The growth of commercial banking, finance and insurance services is the chief feature of the 1970s. Bank deposits increased threefold between 1970 and 1975.

Considerable incentives have been offered to industrialists to establish concerns in the island: 40 per cent investment grants; 40 per cent on commissioning and running in expenditure; loans of working capital up to 50 per cent, grants for approved training courses for employees; and even rent reduction in some cases. Among the criteria governing qualification for assistance were that the proposed development should not diminish the amenities of the Isle of Man; products should have a high added value content; developments should show a high capital investment per employee and a high return on invested capital, and output should be mainly for export.

Industry set up under the government's encouragement schemes has not in all cases succeeded; a certain failure rate is inevitable, as is found not only in the Isle of Man. However, a survey in 1975 found that the economy was now more diversified and that Manx incomes were at, or above, UK level.

The mineral deposits of the Isle of Man are associated with granitic intrusions into the slate massif—mainly at Dhoon, north of Laxey, and at Foxdale, south of St John's and there are numerous subsidiary dykes where mineralisation has occurred. At one time, the island provided 20 per cent of the zinc and 5 per cent of the lead mined in the British Isles, as well as minor amounts of iron, copper, silver, arsenic, antimony and bismuth. The industry dates from medieval times, reaching its zenith in the period 1850–90. In addition to the most important mines at Laxey and Foxdale, there were others at Maughold, on the Calf of Man, and at Bradda Head. The end of the industry was rapid. By 1900 only three mines were left; the last of these, the Great Laxey, closed in 1919. Minerals included galena (lead sulphide), sphalerite (zinc sulphide) and chalcopyrites (copper-iron sulphides). The veins varied in width from inches to 60ft; and their lateral persistence from a few hundred yards to a mile (at Laxey) or $2\frac{1}{2}$ miles (at Foxdale).

The Laxey Wheel

The relics of the defunct mining industry are now part of the landscape. Predominant among them is the famous Laxey

Wheel—the Lady Isabella—one of the best-known and almost certainly the most photographed example of industrial archaeology in the British Isles. Designed by a Manxman, Robert Casement, it was used for draining the mines by pumping out water, and was itself driven by water coming from a cistern higher up on the mountain side, via a 2ft diameter pipe. Laxey Wheel is 72ft 6in in diameter, 6ft in breadth; its shaft is 17ft long by 21in in diameter, weighing nine tons. The wheel is constructed in twenty-four cast-iron segments, on each side, and each segment takes seven buckets. There are forty-eight wooden spokes connecting axle and rim, each of which is 35ft long. The wheel is also strengthened by ninety-six tie rods, each 30mm thick.

A crank at the hub of the wheel imparts a horizontal motion to the shafts connecting the wheel with the pump which it worked. This pump actually raised 250 gallons of water per minute through a height of 1,500ft. The water was not brought right to the surface but was discharged at adit level, whence it descended to emerge further down the valley. The wheel itself revolved at 2½ revolutions per minute.

The Laxey Wheel was purchased by the Manx government in 1965 and has undergone considerable restoration and is now happily working again—superficially at least—in its original condition. Less exotic remains may also be seen in the shape of disused engine houses, particularly in the Foxdale area.

Mining prospects

Formerly there were hundreds of underground workers employed at Laxey and Foxdale. But as long ago as 1911 it was written: 'Since the decay of the Manx mines, there has been an extensive emigration of Manx miners to the gold fields of South Africa and Australia and to various parts of the United States.'

The increasing cost of natural raw materials has led to a reappraisal of mining prospects on the island. In the 1950s

Peel: port and harbour (*Manx Technical Publications*)

Port Erin

Castletown (*Manx Technical Publications*)

considerable work was done in treating some of the dumps in the Snaefell area; and efforts were made to find new mineralised zones, but without reaching positive indication of the presence of ore. In 1962 a comprehensive survey was made by a professional team, for the island's Industrial Officer. The conclusions were discouraging; the cost of searching for ore would be high; quantities were small by world standards, and underground work necessary for recovering the ore. The rising price of lead might make reappraisal necessary in the future; and the possibility was mentioned of obtaining copper from very old workings on Bradda Head.

Coal

No coal measures are known to exist under the island. Searches were made around Peel and in the south-east, near Ballasalla, in the last century. It was also thought that the Cumberland coal measures might be extended to the northern part of the island, but no success was achieved.

Salt

A salt-mining operation was begun near the Point of Ayre in 1902 whereby brine was extracted by percolation of sea water through the underground deposits. The brine was piped to Ramsey where a salt works was set up. Up till World War I about 7,000 tons were produced annually. After the war, production declined till the company went out of business in 1956.

Peat

Peat, formerly cut in the moorlands and in the Curraghs, was the only native fuel in the Isle of Man. The principal turbaries were west of Snaefell, on the northern slopes of Beinn y Phott—the name means turf-mountain—and in the Curraghs of Ballaugh and Lezayre. In the south turf was cut on the east side of South Barrule, for the most part; though there were evidently smaller turbaries dotted about the lower slopes of the mountains. Possibly the energy crisis which was so intensified in 1973 may see renewed interest in peat as a fuel.

Slate and stone

Manx slate occurs in abundance, though it suffers from the disadvantage that it does not yield a true cleavage as does Welsh slate. Nevertheless quarries were opened in the nineteenth century on South Barrule, at Glen Rushen and at Glen Moar. The Glen Rushen quarry employed 120 men in 1863 and Manx slate, whatever its disadvantages, was certainly used to some extent for roofing. On the whole it was considered an inferior building material, but was used, for example, in large planks, for bridging, for gate posts, and as flooring—as in several rooms in Castle Rushen.

The Red Sandstone of Peel has been used for building for a very long time, as attested by the tenth-century round tower on St Patrick's Isle. It was used, particularly in the eighteenth and nineteenth centuries for adding detail to houses built of other materials. It is a rather soft stone of limited durability, and Peel is open to north-westerly winds. The main quarries were at Creg Malin on the north side of Peel Bay; in the late nineteenth century about 2,000 tons were produced annually.

Limestone for agricultural and other purposes is obtained from the south of the island, in the limestone region round Castletown. Formerly it was shipped by sea to the northern parishes and farmers burnt it in their own kilns. Later, kilns were erected near Castletown, at Derbyhaven and Port St Mary. Castle Rushen is built from local limestone and parts of it date from the thirteenth century; Rushen Abbey is also constructed from local material. The limestone quarry at Scarlett provided stone for Castletown station and for the bridges of the southern section of the Isle of Man railway. Today limestone is quarried at Billown, near Ballasalla, in workings dating back over a century.

9   A TOUR OF THE ISLAND

THE coastal perimeter of the Isle of Man measures about 70 miles, omitting the various creeks and indentations which are very numerous, particularly on the south-east coast with its succession of bays. Off the south-west corner is the Calf of Man, separated from the mainland by the Sound, a narrow and turbulent strip of water, which contains also the small islet of Kitterland. The coast is fairly rugged hereabouts, having undergone a change on the south side of Port St Mary, in the area where the south-eastern limestone ends and the slate massif emerges in the form of tall cliffs. Port Erin lies about 2 miles north of the Sound, its semicircular bay looking out to the west as far as the Mourne Mountains in the north of Ireland. On the north side of Port Erin Bay, Bradda Head dominates the scene, capped by Milner's Tower erected to the memory of a local benefactor. The next bay to the north is Fleshwick, nestling between Bradda and the lower slopes of Cronk-ny-Irree-Laa.

From here the coast runs without indentation for several miles, with the cliffs falling precipitously into the sea in an imposing façade. The Niarbyl reef thrusts out to sea eventually and the coast swings round towards Peel, 5 miles farther on. Jutting out a mile or so before Peel Harbour is Contrary Head, so called because the tidal floods meet here, often causing ugly cross seas. Adjoining it is Corrin's Hill, surmounted by Corrin's Folly. Corrin was a nonconformist eccentric in the early nineteenth century who did not wish to be buried in consecrated ground and erected a tower as a future mausoleum for himself and his family; the folly was bought by the government in 1836.

North of Peel are Red Sandstone cliffs with numerous pleasant beaches and caves, soon giving way to the more usual slate and crush conglomerate. From Gob-y-Deigan the hills begin to retreat from the coast, and the cliffs give way to a level sandy shore with brows of sand and gravel. This type of coast persists right round the Point of Ayre and south again to Ramsey, until the foot of the North Barrule is reached. Various rivers break the continuity of the flat northern shores—at Ballaugh; between Ballaugh and Jurby where the Killane river enters the sea, and north of Jurby where the Lhen trench flows out.

At Ramsey, after running south for several miles, the coast bends towards the east, and the slate cliffs begin anew around the Maughold peninsula. Maughold Head is a rounded hill spur, an eastern extension of North Barrule, 373ft high with a 200ft sheer cliff face. From Maughold to Laxey the coast is rugged and fine, perhaps reaching its best at Bulgham Bay, just north of Laxey. There are numerous creeks all along the east coast, such as Port Mooar, Port Cornaa and Dhoon. Laxey Bay is wide and shallow, with Laxey river and harbour nestling at the northern end and Garwick Glen at the southern end. Rounding Clay Head, the coast, always rocky and steep, turns westward; after the inlet of Groudle Glen comes Banks' Howe, and Douglas Bay begins its superb sweep.

From Douglas Head southward there are some magnificent cliff views, now easily accessible to motor traffic on the Marine Drive. The next inlet is at Port Soderick, uninhabited except for summer visitors. Just beyond is Santon Head, where the coast again bends round, this time to the west.

Langness, 3 miles on, is a long peninsula attached to the mainland by an isthmus. At the northern end of the peninsula is a small islet, St Michael's Isle, connected by a causeway to the mainland. Langness is low lying and was formerly the scene of a large number of wrecks, especially of vessels making for

148

Liverpool from the south. The peninsula forms the eastern side of Castletown Bay, which faces almost due south; on the western end is Scarlett Point. The next bay is Bay-ny-Carrickey, or Rocky Bay, containing at its eastern side Poyll Vaaish and its limestone; at the other side is Port St Mary in a little bay of its own, with a very sheltered harbour. From Santon to Port St Mary the coast is low lying, but at Perwick Bay, just beyond Port St Mary, the slate cliffs re-emerge, and the round-the-coast tour ends where it began.

DOUGLAS

Douglas Bay and Promenade present an unrivalled first sight of the Isle of Man. All passenger vessels now arrive at Douglas, and probably a majority of air passengers make straight for the town, so it may quite justifiably be termed 'the gateway of Man'. Although it has now expanded in several directions, the town is basically shaped like an amphitheatre, with fairly steep slopes rising all round the shore line.

The promenade

The last major work on the promenade was carried out in the 1930s when the Loch Promenade, the section nearest to the pier, was widened and sunken gardens were laid down, which in the season are constantly shining with colour. At the end of the Victoria Pier, and within easy reach of the King Edward VIII Pier, is the sea terminal, a building of recognisably modern type containing waiting rooms and a restaurant, where functions are held, particularly in the winter. Outside is Peveril Square, and adjoining it is the Jubilee Clock, marking the junction of the Loch Promenade and Victoria Street. This street was built in the late nineteenth century on the site of part of the original town of Douglas. Along the Loch Promenade—the last section of the promenades to be completed, at the end of last century— the hotels are of more uniform exterior than those on other parts of the seafront; brightly painted and renovated, they present an attractive appearance.

Running just a stone's throw behind the Loch Promenade is the main shopping street, Strand Street. Formerly known as Sand Street, it abutted directly on to the seashore before the promenade and its associated structures existed. At the south, Victoria Street, end it becomes Duke Street and, at the north end, Castle Street, before emerging on to the seafront—hereabouts called the Harris Promenade—at the foot of Church Road. The Anglican church of St Thomas, in Church Road, is distinguished by a strange, squat, pyramidal clock tower—the original intention was to build a tall spire but evidently funds were not forthcoming, even in the mid-nineteenth century. Just beyond Church Road, on the seafront again, is the Gaiety Theatre; its interior is a magnificent piece of Victoriana which it is hoped will be cherished and preserved under government ownership. On the promenade at this point is the War Memorial, commemorating the Manx dead in the two world wars. Whatever feelings they may have had about independence, Manxmen have traditionally shown enthusiastic loyalty to the Sovereign as the Lord of Man.

Almost opposite the memorial is the Villa Marina, an entertainment centre with gardens and bowling greens. There is a fine central hall or ballroom; seating 2,000 it is much used as a conference centre. The Villa stands at the corner of the Harris Promenade and Broadway, which leads quite steeply up to the top of the town. Not so 'broad' as it may have seemed a century ago, it is a busy thoroughfare even in winter, providing access to Upper Douglas and a quick way out of town.

Beyond Broadway, the landward side of the promenade is known as the Crescent. Two old terraces are contiguous here—Clarence Terrace and then the Esplanade—the oldest surviving parts of the original seafront; the other sections, farther on to the north, seem to have been much altered. Castle Mona, once the residence of the Dukes of Atholl and now a hotel, may be seen near the new Palace Hotel and the gambling Casino. The Palace Lido entertainment centre, on the site of the Old Palace which catered for dancing and also had a variety show, provides more modern types of amusement such as a discotheque. Towards the northern end of the promenade, Summer Hill branches off, leading fairly directly to Onchan Village. The promenade, having been the Central Promenade from Broadway onwards, and then the Queen's Promenade, now becomes Strathallen Crescent, another old section of the seafront. Here stood Derby Castle, demolished in the 1960s to make way for a new concept in entertainment centres—the well-known and ill-fated Summerland.

Summerland

The basic idea behind Summerland was 'to create something of a Cornish village atmosphere and activity in an artificial Mediterranean climate'. Such pursuits as seaside shopping, lounging, sunbathing, swimming and listening to minstrels at the end of the pier were to be combined under one roof, impervious to adverse weather conditions, in a building incorporating a good deal of transparency whereby sunlight could illuminate the scene. The original idealised concept was perforce changed into more realistic holiday requirements, such as rock 'n' roll, bingo, amusement arcades and licensed bars. The decision was taken to lease the building to a well-known British catering and entertainment firm, who were given the responsibility for designing the more decorative part of the interior of the structure.

Planning began in 1965, work commenced in October 1968, and Summerland opened in May 1971, though fitting was not complete until the following year. In all, the various floors of the complex gave over 110,000ft of space, and was expected to cater for 3,000–5,000 visitors at any one time. The main structure was destroyed by a disastrous fire, with considerable loss of life, in the summer of 1973—a sad end to an enterprising innovation. The reconstruction of Summerland is currently under discussion. Associated with it was an aquadrome with two heated seawater swimming pools, sauna baths, Russian vapour baths and massage facilities. This escaped the worst of the fire and has continued to operate.

The harbour

The roadway of the promenade continues round the coast passing Onchan Head, site of a funfair in summer, and then curling round over the shoulder of Banks' Howe, and carrying the Manx electric tramlines as far as Groudle and beyond.

Douglas Harbour, even in its much changed modern style, is still a centre of activity and interest. Steam Packet cargo vessels are always to be seen, loading or unloading from the traditional berth on the seaward side of the swing bridge. Inside the harbour there are generally one or more Scandinavian vessels unloading liquid gas; the Ramsey Steamship Company's ships are often to be seen and a great many pleasure craft tie up there. The inner harbour, including the Steam Packet cargo berth, is completely tidal and ships are high and dry at low tide.

At the top of the harbour and facing Athol Street is the railway station; sadly no longer used, it is an interesting essay in red-faced brick, redolent of the late Victorian era. On the north side of the quay are the markets and sundry hotels.

The south quay leads on round to the breakwater or Battery Pier; this is used for unloading in addition to providing some protection for the passenger piers. Both from the Battery Pier and from the south quay roads lead up the side of Douglas Head, allowing the visitor unrivalled views of Douglas Bay and Harbour. At the top is the hotel, a castellated structure over a century old, and nearby the square, pale cube of the radio station. The old Camera Obscura—based on the 'pinhole camera' principle—offers visitors scenes of various parts of Douglas Head.

Fort Anne on the Douglas Head Road, was originally the home of Buck Whaley, a celebrated eighteenth-century Dublin eccentric, who once walked to Jerusalem and back on a wager and a dare. Whaley was reputedly very wealthy, so it is unlikely that he resorted to Douglas for the usual reason in those days—which was to evade one's debtors. Fort Anne was at one time the home of Sir William Hillary, the lifeboat pioneer, and later became a hotel.

Douglas Head Road merges into the Marine Drive, which pursues a twisting course with dramatic cliff scenery to Port Soderick. The former tramway route is now a fine road fit for all traffic.

The town

Victoria Street, which leaves the promenade by the Jubilee Clock, is a shopping area with a number of banks. It crosses Duke Street—which leads into Strand Street—and turns sharply right farther on, becoming the extremely steep Prospect Hill. At the turn, Ridgway Street branches on the left; here are the municipal buildings of the Douglas corporation, and the public library which is open to visitors. Further up Prospect Hill, Athol Street is on the left—an important commercial centre. At the very steepest part of Prospect Hill, a building on the right with Grecian columns decorating it, is the House of Keys, the seat of the island legislature, and of the main government offices.

Hereabouts Prospect Hill becomes Bucks Road, with shops and boarding houses lining it for several hundred yards; it then becomes Woodbourn Road and purely residential. The road runs on almost to St Ninian's Church, which may be regarded as the top of the town, standing on the corner of Ballaquayle and Glencrutchery Roads—the latter, part of the celebrated TT course. Ballaquayle Road is an extension of Broadway, leading up from the seafront near the war memorial. Beyond St Ninian's Church, Ballaquayle Road becomes the Ballanard Road and leads to a considerable new housing development at Willaston. Other such developments are in the area between the Peel and Castletown Roads, near the Quarterbridge; Pulrose was the first modern housing estate in Douglas and there is now a development up the Spring Valley and Castletown Road. Douglas has numerous attractive terraces of Victorian houses. Behind the Gaiety Theatre, the bluff rises sharply and on the top is situated the pleasant façade of Windsor Terrace, perhaps the most attractive of its type in the town. A short distance away, at the top of the dreaded Crellin's Hill, stands the Manx Museum and National Library. These buildings originally formed Noble's Hospital; in the early 1920s it moved to a more promising site, and the museum and library were established there.

The Manx Museum and National Library

The archaeological collection, both of originals and of models, from the important periods of Manx historical development is the main interest of the museum. There is also a fine collection of maps; and a natural history gallery. Folk life exhibits include reconstructed rooms of houses of various types and periods. A small art gallery has pictures by Manx artists and of various island scenes, including early engravings often of historical interest.

The Manx National Library is part of the museum complex and now has its own extension on the most modern lines. The Isle of Man has been the subject of many studies and the task of the researcher was greatly facilitated by the publication in the 1930s of Cubbon's *Bibliography of the Literature of the Isle of Man*. This two-volume work listed all the known books, magazines and articles written about the island from the earliest times. A tremendous debt is owed to William Cubbon who was the National Librarian at the time. In the last forty years the literature has been considerably augmented—few islands, one imagines, can have been written about quite so much! Also available in the library are numerous parish and family records, generally on microfilm; there is a constant stream of visitors using these resources for the purpose of tracing their family ancestry.

Onchan

Once a relatively insignificant village is the nearby thriving and growing township of Onchan, standing above the northern end of Douglas Bay. In Onchan church, Captain Bligh of the *Bounty* was married, on 4 February 1781, to Miss Betham, daughter of the first British customs officer in the island (after the Revestment).

RAMSEY

Ramsey Bay is a wide L-shape, open to the north-east, with the town in the angle of the 'L'. It is generally low lying, though the steep slopes of North Barrule dominate the scene and also serve to shelter the district—it is said that spring arrives here two weeks before the rest of the island. On a hill to the south of Ramsey stands the Albert Tower, a prominent landmark, which was erected to celebrate the unscheduled landing of Queen Victoria and the Prince Consort in 1847, when conditions were too rough for them to go ashore at Douglas.

When the Sulby river at one time flowed out to the north of the present mouth, a small island existed, known as the Mooragh; after the northern exit was dammed and the land reclaimed, all that remained was the lake in the Mooragh Park. On the former 'island' there are residences and a golf course. Besides its harbour, Ramsey boasts the Queen's Pier, which extends almost half a mile from the shore, about 500yd south of the harbour entrance. The pier has been judged unsafe for passenger traffic; the Steam Packet vessels no longer call en route to and from Belfast and Ardrossan, nor is there a direct service to Liverpool. Ramsey harbour is busy enough with a number of small coastal vessels, notably the indigenous Ramsey Steamship Company, and innumerable small pleasure craft. It is completely tidal, with twin lighthouses on either side of the entrance.

Ramsey is a sizeable town which has grown substantially in recent years, with an increasing population of new residents. It has its own grammar school with 600 pupils, and good shopping facilities. Its attractions are natural ones; there is no very imposing architecture. Sea bathing is safe, with good beaches north and south of the harbour. Fishing is available in the noble Sulby river, which is joined just outside the town by the Glen Auldyn river. The town is well situated for walks into the surrounding mountains.

PEEL

Peel, in the west of the island, is often known as the 'sunset city'; the sunsets can be beautiful, with the scarlet orb sinking over the faintly discerned hills of Ireland. Peel is a city of character, with its little twisted streets leading down to the quay and houses of local Red Sandstone. The harbour is essentially that of a small fishing port—fish processing is a big industry here. Along the promenade too the local sandstone is prominent, and red cliffs continue to the north of the town.

'Peel' refers to a stronghold and it seems likely that the history of invasions at this point of the coast gave rise to the town's name. An annual ceremony in July celebrates the first Viking landing in Peel, supposedly in AD798. Local men dressed in Viking costumes, complete with horned helmets, land from a small fleet of what are intended to resemble the original longships. Young ladies are 'abducted', and much fun is had by all.

St Patrick's Isle

Corrin's Hill stands sentinel over the harbour and at its entrance lies St Patrick's Isle—Holmpatrick, as the Vikings called it—which holds so much of the history of the Isle of Man. The islet has been inhabited since prehistoric times, and flint tools and urn fragments have been found. According to tradition, St Patrick landed there in AD444 and spent some time converting the local people—and also banishing the snakes, for which he was so renowned. On the isle are several historic monuments—the Round Tower, with the ruined St Patrick's Church nearby; St German's Cathedral and the ruins of the castle.

The Round Tower

One of the very few existing outside Ireland, it is about 50ft high and 45ft in circumference at the base, and built of local sandstone with hard shell mortar. An earlier drawing shows it with a conical roof—as is usual in the Irish round tower— whereas today it has a flat, castellated one. Dating from the tenth century, the tower has the customary look-outs to the main points of the compass, and the elevated entrance, 7ft from the ground, for security. Like many Irish towers, it is beside the church for whose protection it was built.

St Patrick's Church

The ruined church is partly of contemporary date to the tower, but a good deal of rebuilding was carried out. The west door is closely adjacent to the tower entrance, so that the clergy and their precious treasures could hasten to safety at short notice. This was the parish church of St Patrick of Peel until a new one was built on the mainland in 1714.

St German's Cathedral

The small cruciform church, adjoining the east wall of the castle area, was built on the site of an earlier church; the present building measures 114ft by 68ft at the crossing. Bishop Simon of Argyll, who came to the island in 1226, constructed the original chancel. Other parts of the cathedral were added at various periods, first the tower and transept, then the nave. The 68ft high central tower is square with a staircase bell turret rising above it. Both the tower and the transepts were damaged in the fourteenth century and extensively rebuilt. Red Sandstone seems to have been used for all additions, though it is said that 'some of its light brown stone came from an Ulster quarry'.

In the south-east corner is a piscina—at one time used for washing sacramental vessels. Under the chancel is a crypt which was for centuries the episcopal prison. Those convicted by the ecclesiastical courts for adultery, fornication, cursing and drunkenness were incarcerated there until they did penance for their offences; the last occupant left in 1780.

The Castle Gatehouse

Built by William le Scrope, Earl of Wiltshire and Lord of Man in the fourteenth century, the Red Sandstone structure is in three storeys. Near the ancient entrance door on the right is the guardroom—setting of the story of the famous black dog, or 'Moddey Dhoo', a ghostly black spaniel said to haunt the castle chambers by night. The Bishop's Palace, just north-east of the cathedral, was taken over as the Lord's residence at an early date. The castle at one time had a considerable staff, including armourer, cook, scullions, butler, launderer, plumber, brewer, miller, maltster and swineherd.

On the castle's landward side is a red curtain wall, again of sandstone. On the edge of the rocks on the seaward side is a green curtain wall, of very large slabs of slate, probably built by the first Earl of Derby in the fifteenth century. This wall carries two sally ports and six fortified towers; one is known as 'Fenella's tower' after the famous leap by a character in Sir Walter Scott's *Peveril of the Peak*.

CASTLETOWN

Castletown has its own strong individuality. It has narrow winding streets, a castle and two well-known boarding schools. Nearby is Rushen Abbey and the only remaining vestige of a windmill in the island. Castletown is the home of the Manx Nautical Museum and the site of one of the island's two

158

breweries. The town stands at the mouth of the Silverburn; its rather small harbour is tidal, but there is an outside wharf from which a container service operates to the mainland, and this has put Castletown second, in terms of cargo handled, among the island ports.

Castle Rushen

Situated on the west bank of the Silverburn, where it widens to form the harbour, the castle is a truly remarkable building in that it is so well preserved after 600-odd years of existence. That a castle was sited here may seem a little strange, but Castletown lies amid the best farming country in the island and it would have been natural for the ruler to settle in the locality. Derbyhaven, only a mile or so from the town, was a more favourable place for invaders to land than in Castletown Bay.

An extremely solid structure, the castle was built in the local limestone. Formerly it abutted straight on to the waters of the harbour, but now there is a road in between. It is first mentioned in 1265 when Magnus Barefoot is said to have died in the castle, and it seems likely that Godred Croven built a fortress here in the eleventh century, possibly on the site of a previous Celtic strongpoint. The south and west towers were added later, probably about 1200. After Bruce's invasion in 1313 the castle was repaired and rebuilt.

The first English Lord of Man—William Montacute, Earl of Salisbury—made Castletown his capital, constructing a fortress round the Viking fort; begun in 1334, his son completed the work. The keep now consisted of the Viking fort, with its two towers enlarged with a new eastern tower and a gateway with twin towers. Later in the fourteenth century, a curtain wall with parapet was added, and the keep was raised to enable defenders to fire over the heads of those on the parapet. About 1540, a glacis was built outside the castle moat—as a protection against cannon fire.

159

Adjoining the wall and next to the gatehouse is the Derby House, built at the end of the sixteenth century as domestic quarters by the fifth Earl of Derby. Castle Rushen was used as the centre of government up to the nineteenth century, and at various times as prison, lunatic asylum and barracks. In the rather restricted confines of central Castletown it is difficult to obtain a view of the castle that does it justice. Not placed on an outstanding eminence, it was intended as an entrance door to the island rather than as a dominant and invincible fortress.

Rushen Abbey

Not far from Castletown, though more adjacent to the village of Ballasalla, is Rushen Abbey dating from 1134. Established as a daughter house to Furness Abbey, it was predictably made from the local limestone. The ruins show the abbey to have been cruciform in structure, without any central tower, but a tower over the north transept still remains. Little is left of the south transept or the nave; there is one Norman arch, bricked up, in the chancel. The site of the abbey is most attractive; set beside the Silverburn, it reminds one that medieval abbeys often made great use of water supplies for power generation as well as for domestic and hygienic purposes. The monks here appear to have had two water mills in operation; one may be seen opposite the abbey and the other half a mile upstream.

Museums

The only remaining vestige of a windmill on the island is the Witches' Mill on the outskirts of Castletown. This conical stump is used—perhaps rather ignobly—as a witchcraft museum.

On the east side of Castletown Harbour, slightly downstream of the castle, is the Nautical Museum which occupies Bridge House, the home of the Quayle family. The unique feature of this house is that its basement comprises a boathouse. This was built in 1789–91 to accommodate *Peggy*, the schooner-rigged yacht belonging to Captain Quayle. It was possible to sail her out of the boathouse into the harbour, but in the course of time the exit arch was bricked up and *Peggy* lay undisturbed for over a century. She was rediscovered in 1935 as a survival of the greatest significance, and was to form the central and most outstanding exhibit of the Nautical Museum.

Schools

The educational fund set up by Bishop Barrow in the seventeenth century had prospered, as there was evidently no great desire on the part of young Manxmen to take advantage of the money available to study theology at Dublin University. By 1830 the fund had reached £5,000 and Bishop Ward pressed ahead with a scheme for a school, raising further funds by appeals and by mortgage—the most noteworthy contribution came from King William IV who donated his name! Destroyed by fire in 1844, the school was reconstructed with the help of public subscription. The building, naturally of Castletown limestone, is typical of its period and comparable to British public schools of like age. Standing on the flat lands at Ronaldsway, just outside Castletown, the central tower is a dominating landmark visible from all southern parts of the Isle of Man. Many distinguished Manxmen and others have passed through its classrooms.

In Castletown too is the island's public school for girls, the Buchan School, also founded in the nineteenth century.

PORT ERIN AND PORT ST MARY

The southern tip of the island, including Port Erin, Port St Mary and the peninsula in between, is one of the most fascinating and attractive parts of the Isle of Man. The whole area is presided over by Bradda Head, topped by Milner's Tower. Many years ago housing spread up the side of Bradda Head and from here there are splendid views through the gap into Port St Mary Bay. Port Erin Bay has considerable natural beauty.

Port Erin is the terminus—along with Ballasalla—of what little remains of the Isle of Man Railway. A one-time fishing village, there was at one period some idea of starting a steamer service to Holyhead. However, Port Erin Bay faces due west into the prevailing and strongest winds, and attempts to build breakwaters to shelter the harbour have failed miserably.

A little over a mile away to the south-east lies Port St Mary, or Port le Moirrey; said to be the Manx equivalent of Maryport, it was possibly named after the Blessed Virgin. The basis of this belief is the presence of a small keeil, now buried beneath the town hall, which gives its name to Chapel Beach or Bay. A former fishing port, and undoubtedly a centre of the smuggling industry, Port St Mary is now a harbour for pleasure craft and the headquarters of the Isle of Man Yacht Club. There are two breakwaters: the Alfred Pier to the south and another guarding the harbour, a couple of hundred yards away. Port St Mary Bay, heavily indented, contains within it Gansey Bay as well as Chapel Bay.

National Folk Museum

There is a direct road from Port St Mary to the Sound opposite the Calf of Man. It passes through the village of Cregneish—'the most Manx of villages'. It lies in an idyllic situation and contains the National Folk Museum. This has three components: the Karran Farmstead is a typical crofter's dwelling of former days; Harry Kelly's cottage, about 150 years old, represents the dwelling-house of a fisherman-crofter; and a weaver's cottage, with a hand loom, brought from nearby Ballafesson in 1939. There is also a woodworker's shop, complete with equipment for wood-turning.

Meayll Circle

A road from Port Erin, which joins the road to the Sound at Cregneish, passes just to the west of the Meayll Circle, one of the island's greatest archaeological relics.

A TOUR OF THE ISLAND

The most southerly point of the main island is Spanish Head, so named because of a hypothetical connection with a wreck of a Spanish Armada vessel.

Calf of Man

The Calf of Man was presented to the Manx National Trust in 1937. It is a bird sanctuary and at certain times landing is by permit only. The Calf covers about a square mile and rises to 400ft.

A mile to the south-west is the Chicken Rock, with its lighthouse; it is so called because of its association with storm petrels, or Mother Carey's chickens, which perch there when the rock is exposed.

BIBLIOGRAPHY

GENERAL

As mentioned in the text, Mr W. Cubbon's *Bibliographical Account of Works relating to the Isle of Man* published in two volumes in 1933 and 1939 is central to any account of Manx bibliography. In general, only books published since that time will be cited.

CRAINE, D. *Mannanan's Isle* (1955)
FRASER, MAXWELL. *In Praise of Manxland* (1935, 1948)
STENNING, CANON E. H. *Isle of Man* (1950)
——. *Portrait of the Isle of Man* (1958, 1965)
Journal of the Manx Museum (1924–)

NATURAL FEATURES

BIRCH, J. W. *Climate of the Isle of Man*, VI (IOMNHAS, 1957)
——*The Isle of Man—a Study in Economic Geography* (1964)
CULLEN J. and SLINN D. *Birds of the Isle of Man* (Museum publication, 1975)
FREEMAN, RODGERS and KINVIG. *The Isle of Man in 'Regions of the British Isles—Lancashire, Cheshire & the Isle of Man'* (1966)
GARRAD, Dr L. S. *The Naturalist in the Isle of Man* (1972)
LAMPLUGH, G. W. *Geology of the Isle of Man* (HMSO, 1903)
See also *The Proceedings of the Isle of Man Natural History and Antiquarian Society* New Series (IOMNHAS, 1906), formerly known as *Yn Lioar Manninagh*, 1889–1905

HISTORY

AIRNE, C. W. *Story of the Isle of Man*, 2 vols (1949, 1964)
DEMPSEY, REV W. S. *Story of the Catholic Church in the Isle of Man* (1958)
DILLON, M. and CHADWICK, NORA. *The Celtic Realms* (1967)

BIBLIOGRAPHY

KINVIG, R. H. *The Isle of Man, A Social, Cultural and Political History* (recommended) (1975)
MOORE, A. W. *A History of the Isle of Man* (1900)
WILSON, D. *The Vikings and their Origins* (1970)

MUSEUM PUBLICATIONS

CUBBON, A. M. *Prehistoric Sites in the IOM*
——. *Art of the Manx Crosses*
——. *Ancient and Historic Monuments of the Isle of Man*

CONSTITUTION AND GOVERNMENT

CRAINE, D. *Tynwald* (1976)
The Isle of Man and its relationship to the EEC—a report (1973)
Report of Commission on Constitution (1970)
Report of Mac Dermott Commission (1959)

THE MANXNESS OF MAN

KINLEY, G. Law in the Isle of Man *Bibliographic Guide to the Law of the United Kingdom, Channel Islands and Isle of Man* (1973)
KNEEN, J. J. *Place Names of the Isle of Man*, 6 vols (1925–9)
MOORE, A. W. *Folk Lore of the Isle of Man* (1891, 1971)
——. *Manx Ballads and Music* (1896)
——. *Manx Worthies* (1901)
——. *Manx Names* (1903)
See also Census returns of the island (which may be seen in the National Library)

COMMUNICATIONS

BOYD, J. I. C. *The Isle of Man Railway* (1973)
BROWN, J. 'Harbours of the Isle of Man' *The Dock and Harbour Authority* (May, 1939)
——. *Story of Douglas Harbour*, V (IOMNHAS, 1955)
HENDRY, R. PRESTON and R. POWELL. *Isle of Man Railway Album* (1976)
HENRY, F. *Ships of the Isle of Man Steam Packet Company* (several editions from 1962)

Isle of Man Steam Packet Company Centenary Booklet (1930)
LAMBDEN, W. *Manx Transport Systems* (1964)
PEARSON, F. *Isle of Man Tramways* (1970)
SHEPHERD, J. 'Five Years of Change at Douglas', *Sea Breezes* (April 1972)

VISITING INDUSTRY

The Manx National Library holds a unique collection of visitors guide books from 1822 (Haining) onwards, with many different editions such as Ward Lock's and Black's guides. The Annual Reports of the Tourist Board are now available.

HEAD, Sir G. *A Home Tour through various parts of the United Kingdom* (1837)
HOLLIDAY, BOB. *Racing round the Island* (history of the TT) (1976)
Isle of Man Tourist Development Committee Report (1970)
TOWNLEY, R. *A Journal kept in the Isle of Man* (much the most entertaining account) (1791)
Visiting Industry Commission Report (1955)
WELCH, J. *A Six Days Tour through the Isle of Man* (1836)

INSULAR ECONOMY

The Annual Reports of the various Government Boards are a most valuable source of information.

BAWDEN, et al. *Industrial Archaeology of the Isle of Man* (1972)
BIRCH, J. W. op cit
An Economic Appreciation of the Isle of Man (PA International Management Consultants, 1971)
An Economic Survey (PA International Consultants, 1975)
Mining and Minerals of the Isle of Man (a report to the Industrial Officer) (1962)
SMITH, W. C. *History of the Irish Sea Herring Fishery* (1923)
———. *Review of Herring Fishery in Manx Waters 1923–50*
See also reports on Herring Fishery from the Marine Biological Station

TOPOGRAPHICAL

The Manx Museum, besides publishing valuable information about antiquities, also produces useful guides to nature trails, and various interesting locations.

ACKNOWLEDGEMENTS

THE author is most grateful to the following: Miss Ann Harrison and the staff of the Manx National Library for valuable help most cheerfully given; the Manx Museum for permission to reproduce a number of photographs; the Tourist Board for kindly providing illustrations, and also up-to-date statistics; the Industrial Officer for his help; Dr Larch Garrad for advice on some points; the Isle of Man Steam Packet Company for furnishing information about sailings, and Chris Stillman of Dublin University for help with the geological section. Thanks also to Mr T. Kermeen for advice; to Dr A. R. Brand for help; and to Mr D. H. Hubbard for assistance with photography. All opinions expressed are, needless to say, the author's own for which he accepts full responsibility.

INDEX

INDEX